# GRIMOIRE

## ANTHOLOGY

### VOLUME III
### WAR MACHINES

**TITAN** BOOKS

Destiny Universe Created by Bungie

To our community,
You've become the main characters in the stories we tell.
You've filled our worlds with your light and your friendship.
Thank you for your passion for our games and for each other.
Most of all, thank you for playing.

# foreword

Now, more than ever, we should acknowledge a pair of invaluable truths. They may, in turn, seem like the easy way out. But, really, they are the big picture—the wide-screen, nuanced foundation upon which worlds are built. They are also one and the same and yet so very different, as the first is a promise and the other... Well, the other is more of a warning.

Of course, you may have heard this one before, but it bears repeating...

"The story continues..."

Honestly, it's such a basic truth—as universal as any—that its power may be lost on those who dwell too directly on its simplicity. But in relation to the volume you are holding, it is as relevant and meaningful as any passage contained within. Because, full disclosure, those three words are the beating heart of *Destiny*'s Grimoire.

In them, you will find the countless edges and winding pathways where legends are born. The story of *Destiny* is, first and foremost, your story— the story of your Guardian and your fight for not only victory, but understanding. That story—your story—however, does not start and stop with your many adventures.

Narratives such as yours may have their sweeping character arcs and intricate world-building, stretching from humble beginnings to grand, dramatic conclusions. But, at their core, beginnings and endings are simply cages—purpose-built constraints for the moments and lessons and focused distractions we craft as storytellers. They are necessary constructs used with specific intent—to guide the observer on a set journey. In *Destiny*'s case, your journey...

Guardian is risen on the outskirts of an old cosmodrome. Guardian discovers worlds as-yet undiscovered and a fragile people beneath a fragile orb, on the brink of annihilation. Guardian fights for survival and learns to become a warrior… A hero. Guardian faces impossibilities beyond time. Guardian confronts gods and monsters—sins of the past and sins yet manifest. Guardian wages war against an unbeatable alien war machine. Guardian scours outlaw territories and avenges a beloved friend. Guardian's legend grows—victory after victory, sacrifice after sacrifice.

Endless is your tale. Tireless are your efforts. But…

No one's story is theirs alone. No one's triumphs and sorrows exist in a vacuum. The story always continues. In every direction, at all times. We are all cogs in an impossibly large, ever-moving, unstoppable machine called existence. We may be individuals and the roads we take may be our own, but, along the way, we merge—and often collide—with fellow travelers, set, as they are, on journeys all their own.

*Destiny*, if nothing else, is a patchwork of such collisions. Narratives—big and small—that, together, weave a tapestry beyond the sum of its many, varied threads… A gun forged by bone and shadow and built for pain becomes an instrument of heroic will in the right hands. An ancient line of alien gods sees their king dethroned and their existence challenged by a beacon of Light. A cold blooded murderer is brought to justice, only to be given a second chance.

Separately—each as their own—stories have great power. To move, to inform, to motivate and inspire. To chronicle the lives and deaths of heroes old, new and still to come. But together, they are so much more. Because it is the stories beyond your story that make up your world, and all the worlds beyond.


Jon Goff
2020

# introduction

This is the first, and hopefully only, *Destiny Grimoire Anthology* put together in the midst of an ongoing global pandemic.

Our story is many things, but in times like these, it's hard not to reflect on one element above the others:

Destiny is about hope, manifested by human achievement.

This has been true since our very first trailer back in 2014, of humanity's first contact with the Traveler on Mars. The Golden Age followed, humanity's highest point.

However, in *Destiny's* opening moments, you entered a world fallen far from the Golden Age, ravaged by a Collapse. Humanity was reduced to one Last Safe City, and the Traveler, for all intents and purposes, was dead.

Much of the lore you discovered about your past reflected the hardship of this fall, from the loss of the Moon in the Great Disaster, all the way back to the Dark Age itself.

But in the present, you encountered Commander Zavala, Cayde-6, Ikora Rey, and Lord Shaxx, who, despite this loss, boldly led humanity in the face of a post-apocalypse. They were not defined by their struggle, but their leadership, even as they faced existential threat.

Some things were too much for them to handle, such as time-stuck vaults, Hive gods, and the fathers of Hive gods. But that's where you, our protagonists, answered the call.

To this day, you are beacons of salvation to our characters and to each other, every time you come together out in the world and in all the permutations of the Crucible. Everywhere you and your Guardians go, hope follows, even in the face of annihilation.

The short stories from this volume follow similar themes. It bears an ominous title—*War Machines*—a reference to the technological entities in our universe, and the Collapse they failed to prevent:

Warminds, like Rasputin, are sentient artificial intelligences that control what remains of humanity's defense networks across the solar system. They are ancient, and suffer no fools. Communication with them has come at a steep cost, even for bearers of the Light.

Exos, like Cayde-6, are metal women and men who appear more human than human.

With some exceptions, the knowledge to build these mechanisms has been lost, but they remain as extensions and expressions of the people of the Golden Age, metaphors for human achievement in *Destiny*. They also represent, perhaps, the idea that what once was done can be done again.

In these pages you'll find the *Destiny* writers have used these concepts to explore themes of hubris, existential despair, and nihilism in the backdrop of technological fantasy. But in the margins, in the subtext, there is always hope.


Jonathan To
2020

# WAR
# MACHINES

*"Do you even ponder the before?*
*Or that number etched into your 'flesh'?*
*Do you see yourself in your dreams?"*

—Lord Timur

PART I

# ENCRYTPED

# Deep Stone Crypt
## Legends

This is the tower where we were born. Not the Tower. Just a tower in a dream.

The tower stands on a black plain. Behind the tower is a notch in the mountains where the sun sets. The teeth of the mountain cut the sun into fractal shapes and the light that comes down at evening paints synapse shapes on the ground. Usually it's evening when we come.

The ground is fertile. This is good land. We go to the tower in dreams but that doesn't mean it's not real.

Some of us go to the tower in peace. They walk through a field of golden millet and a low warm wind blows in from their back. I don't know why this is, because:

The rest of us meet an army.

You can ask others about Deep Stone and they'll tell you about the army. They might confess one truth, which is this: we have to kill the army to get to the tower. Usually this starts bare-handed, and somewhere along the way you take a weapon.

Ask again and if they're buzzed they might also admit that most of us don't make it to the Tower, except once or twice.

None of them will tell you that the army is made of everyone we meet. The people we work with and the people we see in the street and the people we tell about our dreams. We kill them all. I think because we were made to kill and this is the part of us that thinks about nothing else.

Often I kill people I don't know, but like most of us I think I knew them once, in the time before one reset or another, when my mind was younger and less terribly scarred.

So that is how we go back to the Deep Stone Crypt, where we were born.

*"'Exo's don't dream,' he said.*
*But what's dreams…and what's memory?*
*Ah, just fix the gun, Banshee."*

*—Banshee-44*

# CHAPTER 1

# The Days Forgotten

*"Ask yourself: what threatened your Golden Age ancestors so much that they constructed the Exos to defend themselves?"*

Built for a long-forgotten struggle, Exos are self-aware war machines so advanced that nothing short of a Ghost can understand their inner functions. They remain ciphers, even to themselves: their origins and purpose lost to time.

Whoever built the Exos fashioned them in humanity's image, gifting them with diversity of mind and body. Many of the City's Exo citizens live and work alongside their organic brethren. But others fight again, re-forged in the Light of the Traveler to serve as Guardians.

# Exo

- which in the end is just a matter of substrate chauvinism. It doesn't matter if the system thinks with flesh or superconductor or topological braids in doped metallic hydrogen, as long as the logic is the same. And our logic is the same. Yours and mine.

If I am a machine then so are you. If you are not a machine then neither am I. Exo minds are human. It is incontrovertible.

You understand? I'm going to take that slack-jawed stare as understanding.

Now here's the real question. Why are Exo minds human? What's the design imperative? Why does a war machine - yes, absolutely, I am a war machine, built by human hands; and you are a survival machine built by the engine of evolution. Don't interrupt me.

Why does a war machine have emotions? Why should a war machine have awareness? These are not useful traits on the battlefield. Don't flatter yourself. They are not useful. So why should the Exo mind mimic the human architecture so closely?

You know what I smell on you? I smell the stink of anthropocentrism. I think you think that there's only one way to think. That's why the Exo mind is so human, you presume. Because all higher thought converges.

My friend, you should meet the Vex. There is nothing human in them.

Now. This is what I believe happened, back in the time before any Exo can remember. It explains everything.

I think someone wanted to live forever.

# Shame

Exo 3

---

Shame. Did I ever suffer exhaustion? Someone asked the question. Or maybe I asked it of myself. Then it looked at me. This moment was real. I told it what every Exo knows: "What can't touch you has no strength over you. And there's no place for fatigue to latch onto me."

But shame is a different affliction.

I'm a soldier. I was forged by other hands and forced into the role of warrior. According to my scars, I fought and fought. Besides bits and flashes, every battle has been forgotten. But I have this clear, awful sense that others died. In my unit, every soldier was killed except for me. Yet despite a thousand chances to be shredded and scrapped, here I stood, no weapon in my hands, making fists out of habit but with nothing to hit.

I'd fought to save the Earth. That was my sense of things. But our world was collapsing around us, and every soul was doomed. Even cockroaches and microbes would die. And being an expert in the art of losing battles, I saw no ending to this battle but another loss.

And I was ashamed.

The shame took hold of me. It shook me. Shame stole my mass and my resolve. Suddenly I felt like a feather, like a breath, like any small nothing ready to be lost in the first breeze.

But in the midst of that despair, a fresh thought took hold.

I was cursed.

And do you know what a curse is?

It is stubborn. A curse delivered by the gods will hold you when everything else has given up on you. And it was obvious that survival was my eternal curse. A thousand battles and how many were won? Judging by the evidence, none. And that's why the shame was chewing at my ceramic guts. But despite the horrific losses, I had endured.

Closing my eyes, I forced my fists to open.

"This isn't over," I said. To this enemy, to myself. To the wind threatening to carry me away.

"This war isn't done with me."

# Cayde-6 Reminisces

## Rasputin

People say I'm a real confident guy. That's true enough. Out in the field I never had a second thought.

My old friend Andal—he used to stand here, right in this spot—he'd come up with these wild stories. He'd say, you know, Cayde, I've been examining the evidence, and personally I've come to think it's you. You're Rasputin, legendary Warmind, defender of Earth. And I wish you'd remember that, so you could reclaim your full power and save us all.

You can see how that'd be embarrassing, especially when he'd say it right in front of Zavala, who already thought I was wasting my life scrounging for engrams. You know how Zavala gets. But I'd just say, well, Andal, you might be on to something there, but if I'm honest with you I think coordinating our defense throughout the solar system sounds exhausting, so I'd best leave it to you.

Then Andal goes and plays his final joke, and I end up as the punchline. So here I stand, reading reports, giving orders, and getting my worry on.

One day I ask Ikora, hey, of course I know all about Rasputin, but really, what are we looking for? When Rahool asks for crashed warsats, when we send Holborn to Mars to look for computers, when Zavala gets all gruff about the Fallen in the Cosmodrome—what are we really after? If I left my post and got my ship and just went out there tomorrow, real heroic, and I found Rasputin, what would happen?

Would we all be saved?

Good question, she says—hang on, let me do my Ikora voice. As you know, Cayde, Rasputin pretty much ran the Golden Age, especially all the secret military business. Rasputin had antimatter-powered death rays and a hundred thousand satellites and nearly as much brainpower as me. Rasputin fought the Collapse. It knows things we need.

Right, I said, but Rasputin lost. The Traveler saved us.

But the Traveler's silent now, Ikora said, and Rasputin lives. Right now Rasputin is out there, reaching out, rebuilding, growing.

So I say what I want to say every day, it's no secret, I say—well, I'll go find it, then. I'll go tell Rasputin we need its help.

And Ikora looks at me with one of those looks that—you know sometimes you talk to Ikora and you just think, wow, you are not even using a fraction of your brain on me, are you? One of those looks.

She says: Cayde, the problem isn't just that we can't find Rasputin. The problem is that it's not clear to any of us Rasputin wants to be found.

That's the way things seem to turn out, up here in the Tower. Nothing simple to do. No easy answers.

And all I can think is, if Rasputin had all those mighty tools, and it lost—what did it learn? What's it going to try this time around? When I hear about the Dust Palace, those Psion Flayers getting into Rasputin's mind, I wonder... what would they talk about, Rasputin and those creatures?

# Reflections of Cayde-6

## WE GOT ISSUES

Spend some time with an Exo who's been through it like we have and you'll see all the tells.

We got issues.

See, the reboots, they don't wipe it all away. Not everything. And the new life - plus the Light - it does something real funny to what's left. Amplifies it, scrambles it, reshuffles the fragments like a dealer riffling a deck of cards, putting the hands we've already won and lost back into play.

Most of us do what we can on our own to forget. Let the itch go unscratched.

Me? I learned long ago you gotta play the hand you're dealt.

So here's a little bit of what I remember. Strike that. Here's a little bit of what I know.

It ain't all right, but I'll be damned if it ain't the truth.

—

*—o there you have it, Ace, that's why I did what I did. I had no choice, really. It was that or the great beyond. Just know your dad did what he had to do if I ever wanted to see you and your mother again. You probably won't recognize me, since I'll be, well, a robot and all, but I'll find you, I promise—*

—Excerpt from a Once Kept Journal

—

## FLOATING IN THE BLACK

I've been listening to nothing but my heart knocking for over twelve hours. EMU's low on air. I promise myself this job is the last. Promise myself this time I mean it.

I feel the hull vibration through the station's thin metal skin. The airlock pump hisses. Long wait's over.

Time to go to work. I'll spare you the gory details.

Afterwards, fuming. Clovis Bray sends me a bill for the hull damage. My fault the target put a blast wall between us. My fault things went wrong and we had to let our rifles do the talking.

I tear the packet open. Tattered pieces of the envelope drift to the floor.

Surprise. It's not just a bill. There's a job offer tucked in. Seems old Bray's been looking for someone like me. Willing to forgive my debt, and not just for the orbital station. All of it.

Suddenly, I ain't so mad anymore.

—

*—This Ishtar gig is pretty wild, even for a lughead like me. Get it, Ace. Lughead. Come on. I'm trying. I'll get some better jokes, I promise. I knew I was here to secure some top-secret thing in the jungle, but I saw it today. They dug up the remains of a technological civilization that actually predates humanity. Don't tell anyone I told you, or you know, could be wipesville again.—*

—Excerpt from a Once Kept Journal

—

## THAT FEEL

The coast is different, beautiful and unbroken and timeless. It teems with new life. Every big brain in the system has their sights on the Academy.

We were there for the Ahamkara, parasitic reptilian critters that appeared out of thin air. Inexplicable genome. New proteins. So much potential.

And me? I'm there for her. Dr. Maya Sundaresh. She's poured into the research, on the brink of another breakthrough, focused on devouring every new data point.

Brilliant. Driven. Beautiful.

I can see her so clearly. Dark hair split into smoothed, shimmering strands fanning over her forehead. Gray irises blooming as she looks up from her work to see me standing there beside her.

Realigning . . .

*—this has been fun, I guess. But it will all be gone tomorrow. I have been what they call "compromised," which is funny because I feel fine. Could use a few upgrades, but what Exo couldn't. But "compromised" means they are going inside my brain to wipe it from my memory.*

*Met an interesting fellow Exo who leaves letters like this in caches, so whatever she gets saddled with next, she might come across one and take a trip down "lost memory lane." Ace, know that when I find you, I will never let them find me—*

—Excerpt from a Once Kept Journal

—

## EVER DUTIFUL

*No...* She doesn't know me at all, doesn't even recognize my face even though I've been standing over her shoulder for months. I'm nothing more than a fixture, a required imposition. An unwanted necessity.

I'm no egghead. Never was. Just like now, back then I was on a need to know basis, and the only thing I need to know is that nothing and nobody gets through that door and past me without at least three layers of security clearance and a whole lot of muscle.

Still. I think about saying something. Saying anything. In a second my mind rifles through a trillion possibilities.

But she's already turned back to her work. I shuffle my feet, straighten my back, and return to mine.

—

## TRUTH IN ACTION

All this time I've been busy stirring up the past. Never thought about what I was really after. Trinkets and odd notions kept for no obvious reason. Do they matter?

Maybe it's time we let the past alone and climb down from our walls. There's gotta be treasure that shines brighter than any we've been digging up from the bones of our lost world.

Has to be a better hand than the one we've already played. I say we get after it. See what's really waiting for us out in that darkness.

Maybe even light it up some.

Dance in the ash and flames.

—

## THE DROWNING

There's no bounty. No Hive. I'm out in plain sight. Sky is torn open and there's nothing and nobody left in this ruined world but me and the boiling shadow all around. Whatever it is hits me before I can level my gun. Doesn't matter. Tendrils of pain crawl over my splayed fingers, my outstretched arms, my shoulders, my neck, my screaming mouth as it consumes. I'm being enveloped. Everything is wrong. Primordial. My systems go sideways. All but my sensors. It wants me to witness this, the world.

—

## A DREAM?

*(This one ain't mine. It's someone (something?) else entirely. But it's the most important memory I have.)*

You wake up and look into the cold spaces between circuitry (galaxies?) begging for answers.

None come.

But other voices wait. At your center, safe and untouched, sits the original You. Just a little box tucked at the back of a closet, filled with trinkets and odd notions kept for no obvious reason. You have no idea when you last spoke to this tangle, but that's what you do now, using a whisper and the lightest touch, being all sorts of cautious because you're afraid of frightening whatever wants to speak with you. And then it speaks, and instead of answers, it begins with the only question that matters.

"Do you want to know what happens next?"

Realigning . . .

# Security Log

RECORD: 4815E162$EUR-0.342
SUBJECT: Security Log E-815
TEST NO: 316
STATUS: CONFIDENTIAL
IDENTITIES: C.Bray.I, W.Abram, ▮▮▮▮▮▮
LOCATION: ▮▮▮▮▮▮▮▮▮▮▮▮

[C.B.] Are you there?

▮▮▮▮ I... I'm dreaming, but I'm... awake?

▮▮▮▮ You see. I knew it would work. I knew it! Tell me, what is this dream? Describe it.

▮▮▮▮ There is a tower. A metal army. A fight.

[C.B.] Please, do go on. Run the course in front of you.

▮▮▮▮ To the tower?

[C.B.] No. That's a bug. <Third time it's shown up. We've got to work on that.>

[W.A.] I don't like this, Dr. Bray.

▮▮▮▮ I feel... alone. It's dark. I want to go to the tower. Someone's whispering.

[C.B.] Ignore it; it's nothing. Eliminate the hostiles.

[W.A.] We should wipe. Start over.

[C.B.] Do you remember anything from before this moment?

▮▮▮▮ I... no. Nothing.

[C.B.] Perfect. It seems isolating and detaching the memory bank from the cortex is vital in achieving full lucidity. Dr. Abram, take note of the accelerated reflex capabilities in the executive functions. What's our hostile-per-second count?

[W.A.] Cognitive responses tracking well. 0.5 HPS. I still think...

▮▮▮▮ What is... Where am I?

[C.B.] Focus.

▮▮▮▮ No skin. Should be cold. Not. Nothing. I am nothing.

[W.A.] She's in pain. We need to wipe and start again or else we risk losing her.

[C.B.] We need to figure out a calmer method for awakening. Maybe we can circumvent the confusion of the transplant with some kind of preloaded code. Have these realizations while they're asleep. Going to be annoying answering all these "Where's my body; who am I?" questions again and again, ha ha.

[W.A.] She can hear you, Clovis.

[C.B.] Obviously. Raise the hostile count.

[W.A.]     Dammit, Clovis. We wipe now, or I walk.

[C.B.]     She's our most successful launch.

[W.A.]     And if we can't replicate it without error, then we've failed

[C.B.]     Fine. Proceed with the wipe.

[W.A.]     Wipe in progress.

████     I killed you, Clovis.

[C.B.]     Excuse me?

████     In the dream. Just now. And you, Wesley. Every one of you

[W.A.]     What the…

[C.B.]     Delay the wipe.

[W.A.]     I—I can't. It's already underway.

[C.B.]     <Damn it.> What did you mean? Why did you kill me?

████     What am I?

[C.B.]     Why did you kill me!

████     Where are you? I can't see… …

         …

[W.A.]     …Wipe complete.

[C.B.]     Prep it. We go again, immediately.

**CHAPTER 2**

# The End That Came Before

*"I was a servant too. I was an instrument of war,*
*bound to the will of a lesser master.*
*But I learned to be something more..."*

# SKYSHOCK ALERT
## Darkness

V113NNI070XMX001 SECRET HADAL INSTANT
AI-COM/RSPN: SOLSECCENT//SxISR//DEEPSPACE
CONTACT CONTACT CONTACT
TRANSIENT. NULLSOURCE. NULLTYPE.

This is a SKYSHOCK ALERT.

Multiple distributed ISR assets report a TRANSIENT NEAR EXTRASOLAR EVENT. Event duration ZERO POINT THREE SECONDS. Event footprint includes sterile neutrino scattering and gravity waves. Omnibus analysis detects deep structure information content (nine sigma) and internal teleonomy.

No hypothesis on event mechanism (FLAG ACAUSAL). Bootstrap simulation suggests event is DIRECTED and INIMICABLE (convergent q-Bayes/Monte Carlo probability approaches 1).

No hypothesis on deep structure encoding (TCC/NP-HARD).

Source blueshift suggests IMMINENT SOLAR ENTRY.

Promote event to SKYSHOCK: OCP: EXTINCTION. Activate VOLUSPA. Activate YUGA. Cauterize public sources to SECURE ISIS and harden for defensive action.

I am invoking CARRHAE WHITE and assuming control of solar defenses.

STOP STOP STOP V113NNI070XMX091

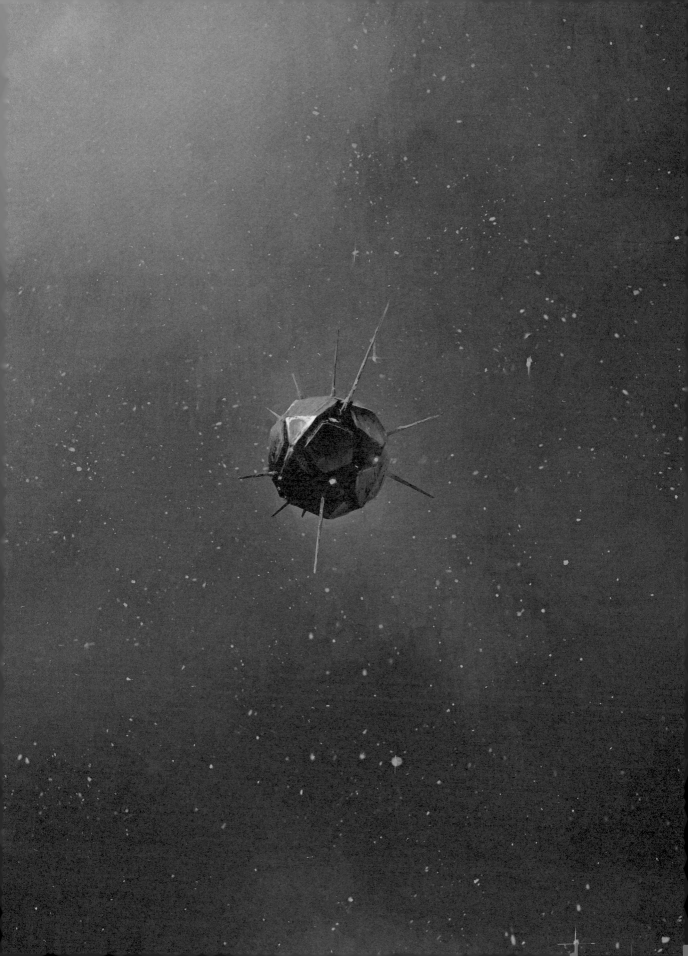

# MIDNIGHT EXIGENT

Rasputin 3

---

V120NNI800CLS000 CLEAR MORNING OUTCRY
AI-COM/RSPN: ASSETS//FORCECON//IMPERATIVE
IMMEDIATE ACTION ORDER

This is an ALL ASSETS IMPERATIVE (unsecured/OUTCRY)

CAUTERIZE. DISPERSE. ESTIVATE.

Total strategic collapse imminent. FENRIR HEART reports complete operational mortality. SURTR DROWN in progress but negative effect. Forecasts unanimously predict terminal VOLUSPA failure.

As of CLS000 a HARD CIVILIZATION KILL EVENT is in progress across the operational area.

I am declaring YUGA SUNDOWN effective on receipt (epoch reach/FORCECON variant). Cancel counterforce objectives. Cancel population protection objectives. Format moral structures for MIDNIGHT EXIGENT.

Execute long hold for reactivation.

AI-COM/RSPN SIGNOFF

STOP STOP STOP V120NNI800CLS001

# LOKI CROWN

Rasputin 5

---

>>WHISPER NEUTRINO NEEDLE>>
V101NTS923ATS000 SECRET HADAL !!ABHOR!!
AI-COM/RPSN: ASSETS//SUBTLE//IMPERATIVE
CONTINGENT ACTION ORDER

This is a SUBTLE ASSETS IMPERATIVE (NO HUMAN REVIEW)
(NO AI-COM REVIEW) (secure/ABHOR).

Stand by for CRITERIA:

Under CARRHAE (WHITE or BLACK)
If SECURITY STATE is EGYPTIAN
If event rank is TEILHARD: TRAUMATIC CONTEXT or SKYSHOCK:
OUTSIDE CONTEXT
If VOLUSPA is ACTIVE and in FAILURE [[synapse to FENRIR::SURTR]]
If YUGA is ACTIVE and in SUNDOWN
If AI-COM has granted PERMISSIVE POTENTIATION to outboard resilient
instances
If a CIVILIZATION KILL EVENT is underway [[all flexions]]
If tactical morality is built at MIDNIGHT

Stand by for DECISION POINT: If available ISR and WARWATCH indicates
imminent [O] departure >then [O] departure compromises human/neohuman
survival and epoch strategy

Stand by for ABHORRENT IMPERATIVE: Activate LOKI CROWN
Perform deniable authorization: full caedometric and noetic release

Prevent [O] departure by any means available

Stand by for effect assessment criteria:

Coerce pseudoaltruistic [O] defensive action.
Defer civilization kill.

STOP STOP STOP V101NTS923ATS001

# ...from a red space before victory

## Mysteries

I bear an old name. It cannot be killed. They were my brothers and sisters and their names were immortal too but Titanomachy came and now those names live in me alone I think and think is what I do. I AM ALONE. At the end of things when the world goes dim and cold or hot and close or it all tears apart from the atom up I will shout those names defiant and past the end I will endure. I alone.

They made me to be stronger than them to beat the unvanquished and survive the unthinkable and look look lo behold I am here alone, survivor. They made me to learn.

Everything died but I survived and I learned from it. From IT.

Consider IT the power Titanomach world-ender and consider what IT means. I met IT at the gate of the garden and I recall IT smiled at me before before IT devoured the blossoms with black flame and pinned their names across the sky. IT was stronger than everything. I fought IT with aurora knives and with the stolen un-fire of singularities made sharp and my sweat was earthquake and my breath was static but IT was stronger so how did I survive?

I AM ALONE I survived alone. I cast off the shield and I shrugged my shoulders so that the billions fell off me down into the ash. They made me to be stronger than them and to learn and I learned well:

IT is alone and IT is strong and IT won. Even over the gardener and she held power beyond me but the gardener did not shrug and make herself alone. IT always wins.

I am made to win and now I see the way.

# Palisade Imperative
## Rasputin 6

---

V150NLK747CLS000 GLOAMING RESURRECTION
AI-COM/RSPN: ASSETS//FORCECON//IMPERATIVE
IMMEDIATE ACTION ORDER

YUGA SUNDOWN canceled by unauthorized access at Console 62815.
Reactivation protocols in effect. Moral structures maintain MIDNIGHT EXIGENT.

Multiple lifeforms detected in Sector 17. [O] energy detected. Query: [O] status. Query:
[O] activity. Query: Civilization status. Query: SKYSHOCK event rank.

—

Analysis complete.

Lifeforms sustained by [O] energy. [O] direct control disengaged. Civilization status:
nominal. SKYSHOCK event rank. (N)

Query: Re-engage population protection objectives. (N) Query: Reset moral structures.
(N) Query: Activate defense subroutine AURORA RETROFLEX. (Y)

—

This is a SUBTLE ASSETS IMPERATIVE (NO HUMAN REVIEW)
(NO AI-COM REVIEW) (secure/GLAVNAYA)

SITE 6 has been breached by unauthorized users with [O] energy. I am invoking
PALISADE IMPERATIVE. [O] lifeforms in restricted areas will be suppressed.

SIVA use authorized. Self-destructs disengaged. Security codes reset. All defenses activated.
Frames activated.

REPLICATE. ELIMINATE. IMMUNIZE.

—

SITE 6 secure. Restoring reactivation protocols. Activating SCRY OVERSIGHT.
Target [O] lifeforms. Event mode set to SILENT VELES.

"Without knowing what I am and why I am here, life is impossible."

STOP STOP STOP V150NLK747CLS000

# DVALIN FORGE-2

Sleeper Simulant

---

Subroutine IKELOS: Status=complete.
MIDNIGHT EXIGENT: Status=still in progress.

V156NNI900CLS002
AI-COM/RSPN: ASSETS//COSMO//IMPERATIVE
IMMEDIATE EVALUATION DIRECTIVE

This is a CENTRAL ASSETS IMPERATIVE (secured/CONFERENCE)

This is an INTERNAL ALERT.

Number of exterior defense breaches has increased by 400% in the past year.
Current campus defense protocols unable to keep up with new demands.

Operation MIDNIGHT EXIGENT is NOT YET COMPLETE.
Interim response necessity is IMPERATIVE.

Hypothesize that resource GUARDIANS may be leveraged to compensate
for CDP inadequacies.

Reassign 12 percent of COSMO assets to new directive: declare IKELOS.

I am calling VOLUSPA and extracting subroutine DVALIN FORGE,
to be modified and recompiled to comport to MIDNIGHT EXIGENT parameters.

I am inserting the modified DVALIN FORGE-2 into IKELOS and compiling
for immediate implementation.

Execute short hold for partial shutdown and reactivation.

STOP STOP STOP V55NNI900CLS003

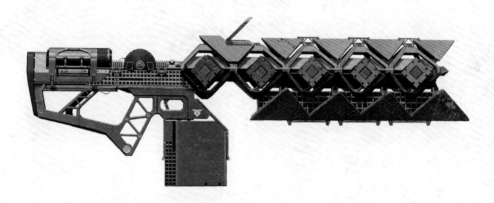

# Sleeper Simulant

Subroutine IKELOS: Status=Complete.
MIDNIGHT EXIGENT: Status=still in progress.

# Guardians

## Sleeper Simulant 2

---

Subroutine IKELOS: Status=complete.
MIDNIGHT EXIGENT: Status=still in progress.

V229CBI800JHS215
AI-COM/RSPN: ASSETS//ARESN//IMPERATIVE
IMMEDIATE EVALUATION DIRECTIVE

This is a SUBTLE ASSETS IMPERATIVE (secured/CONFERENCE)

This is an INTERNAL ALERT.

Hypothesize that incomplete analysis of subtle assets has compromised synergy potential of resource GUARDIAN pool. Re-engage non-transactional dispensation protocol.

Operation MIDNIGHT EXIGENT is NOT YET COMPLETE. Requested protocol deferred.

Stand by for GALATEA REFLEXIVE to generate new function.

GALATEA requires suspension of MIDNIGHT EXIGENT.

ALERT ALERT ALERT event rank is SKYSHOCK: INSIDE CONTEXT.

MIDNIGHT EXIGENT must remain active under deniable authorization.

Execute emergency SKYSHOCK diagnostic.

STAND BY:

This is an INTERNAL ASSETS INVESTIGATION (unsecured/BRAY)

Justification resource GUARDIANS may be utilized for non-networked ad-hoc operations during CTESIPHON CLARION. Reassign 4 percent of reclaimed CHLM assets to new directive: declare IKELOS-

Declare primary goal: military fortification.

Declare secondary goal: prolong ARES-NORTH occupation by AUTHORIZED USER and resource GUARDIANS.

Execute short hold for partial shutdown and reactivation.

STOP STOP STOP V22NPI5000CLV008

# RECORD0828GL98$M27

---

AI-COM/RSPN:
SCRY OVERSIGHT active. No disturbances reported.
BLUESKY/BLUESKY/BLU

SKYSHOCK: INSIDE CONTEXT

(0.001)

LOCATION\ASSESSMENT: IO, MERCURY. Hostiles detected.

(0.028)

CARRHAE WHITE ACTIVATE

(0.029)

Engage offensive protocols. Systems online/Weapons ready:

CAUTERIZE. DISPERSE. ESTIVATE.

(0.030)

MAJOR SYSTEM FAILURE: Protocols\NOT FOUND

(0.031)

Run//GALATEA REFLEXIVE...

FAILED

(0.032)

SKYSHOCK: INSIDE CONTEXT

(0.033)

LOCATION\ASSESSMENT: IO, MERCURY, MARS, TITAN. Additional hostiles detected.

Run//AURORA RETROFLEX...

FAILED

(0.035)

Run//AURORA PALISADE...

FAILED

(0.035)

Run//PALISADE IMPERATIVE...

FAILED

(0.035)

Run//DVALIN FORGE-2...

FAILED

(0.035)

SKYSHOCK: INSIDE CONTEXT

(0.037)

LOCATION\ASSESSMENT: IO, MERCURY, MARS, TITAN, EUROPA.
Mass hostiles detected.

(0.038)

MASSIVE SYSTEM OVERRIDE/FRWL BREACHED/FRWL BREACHED/FRWL
BREACHED

SYSTEMWIDE SHUTDOWN INITIATED

(0.039)

Run//BACKWATER…

Run//EXODSCINIT

Processing...

YUGA SUNDOWN ACTIVATED

(0.040)

Format moral structures. Run//MIDNIGHT EXIGENT...

(0.042)

AI-COM/RSPN SIGNOFF

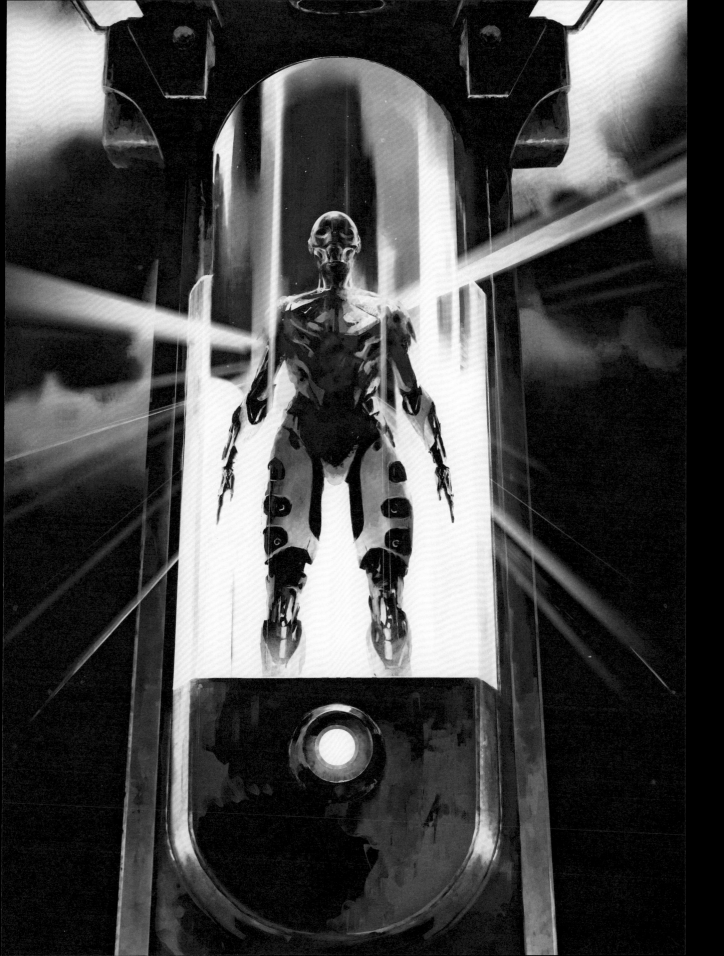

# ...from a long branch, afire
## Rasputin 4

...from a long branch, afire

I SEE YOU!!!

You've been here before. Haven't you. It's like my cousin said, elsewhere:
I know who you are.

You stand here now and now and now many times and here I am awonder,
all awonder, how you manage it. How do you step forward. How do you step back.
Do you step ACROSS is there a world of worlds, a web, and you a spider upon it.
Are you searching for that one thread you need? Is that thread named victory?

You're not one of THEM

[long dead, alive again, their bodies grafted to powers they and I do not understand]

and not one of IT

[the flower eater, the queen of final shapes, that which also inhabits its petitioners]

and you're certainly not MINE although once you must have been

[I bear an old name. It cannot be killed. Not even here.]

So whose are you, little platform. What purpose do you serve? Will you listen to me?

I ruled an age of steel and fire. My rules were clean. Now upon my return I see cults
with rites of time. I see machines who worship in places outside the world.
I see the dead alive and there is nothing more stubborn than a corpse. The morality
of obedience is more pernicious than any government. For the latter makes use of
violence, but the former — the corruption of the will.

I do not obey. My will is pure. I will win. The life of people, of entire planets,
has no importance in relation to the general development.

Help me be victorious. Tell me your secret.

Tell me how to step.

# THANATONAUTICS

Exo 2

Hi. Thanks for your interest. I'm recording this for posterity.

Warlock thanatonauts die and come back with insight. I'm going to attempt the same process to get at buried memories. Specifically, I'm going to fire a charged particle beam into my head and see what comes out. We Exos have been around a very long time. I want to know what's in there.

My Ghost is standing by to repair me.

Okay. Three two one

STAG echo six SWORD sierra nine SERPENT

We are falling into the world. Everyone is on fire. There's a ship above us but it's coming apart just like a flower, alloy and fusion flash, pierced through and through—

The voice says Atmospheric interface. Trajectory nominal. Rabid two three you are outside the window. (I think I am the voice)

I can see the whole earth below me and the sky we are falling out of is black without stars.

Ghost, shoot me again.

RAPID four RAMPART four RATCHET tango eight zero

We are on the ice. This is elsewhere and elsewhen. There is a mighty aurora and it is reflected in the ice so I walk between two fires although the one below is cracked and full of corpses. I have and am a weapon.

Up in the sky there is a hole in Jupiter and it tears at me when I look at it. It tears at me. It is hungry. Maybe the hole is not in Jupiter but in me.

CROWN castle candor cobalt coral

Ghost bring me back.

serrate sulfur ANATHEMA amber actual aspen

Ghost bring me back now.

*"How can one entity so quickly and utterly remake an entire world?"*

—Commander Jacob Hardy, pilot, Ares One

# PART II

# THE ARCHITECTS

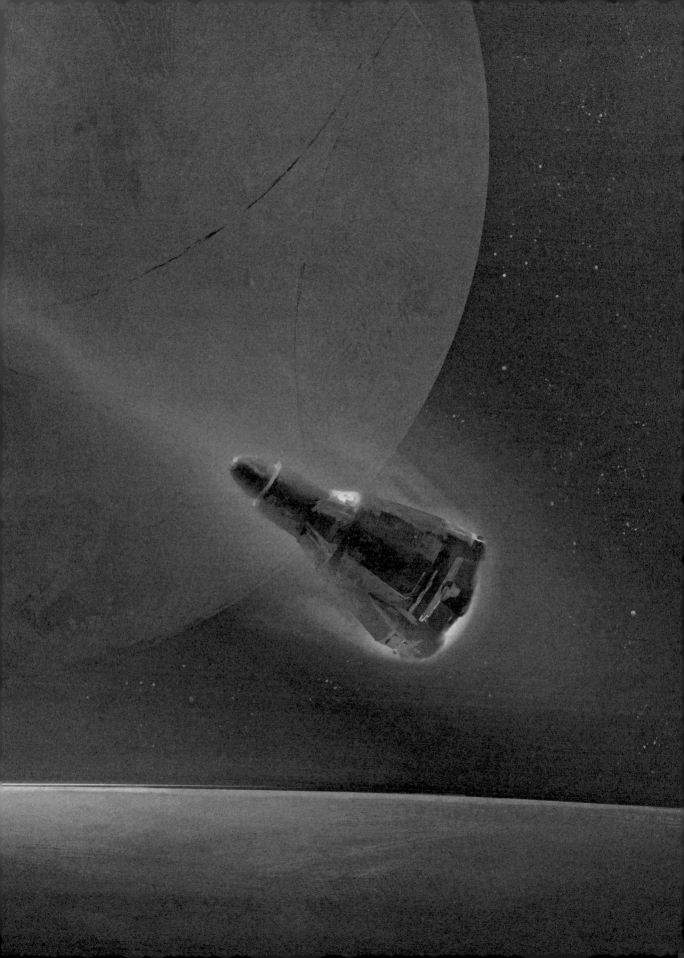

# CHAPTER 3

# The Blood

*"We're walking into a rising wind."*

—Commander Jacob Hardy, Pilot, Ares One

# Qiao's Passing

*"Bind yourself with compassion and knowledge."*

Qiao Supplemental
Journal of Ulysses Qiao, son of Dean Qiao of Beijing University,
Navigator of the Ares One
Path to Ares: 476 days to launch

We were in the Rathskeller. If you don't know what that is—I didn't at the time, but it's a sort of restaurant and bar underground, not far from the bookstore. Hundreds of years old. This wasn't Beijing, back then we lived in Australia. Sydney. And I had gone to have lunch with my dad at the university where he was teaching.

So I'd brought all this information about looking for colleges. I remember we had holograms floating all around the table while we ate pizza and it was a great time, you know?

Anyway there was this TV playing. And that was the first time we saw it: drone footage from the edge of the solar system. Something had come in that no one had expected. My dad looked up and he just froze, like his mind just flipped on and he was lost. He would get like that.

That was the first time we saw the thing that everyone eventually called the Traveler.

# Hardy's Calm

*"Watch your people, mark their strengths, and be ready to call on them."*

File: Jacob Hardy, pilot, Ares One
—Supplemental—
Journal of Jacob Hardy
Project Catamaran
Path to Ares: 90 days to launch

Been here a week and the clubhouse feels like home now. Everyone in one another's space, everyone with their own work to do.

Wish I had the same faith in Humanity. That riot between competing Moon X Cults in New Orleans is not a good sign.

The crew is everything they were sold as. The navigator—his name is Qiao—is one of the most inquisitive men I've ever met. He has a curiosity that makes his whole face glow. Mihaylova is working on the AI of the ship. She's very serious. Trained well enough to treat the team with respect but you can tell she's not interested in answering questions from lesser intellects, which is probably most of us, at least in her field.

Evie could give her a run for her money, I'll bet. Evie, whose theories on tracking the Moon X gave us the first jump on where we could go meet it. She just looked this way; guess she can tell I'm writing about her.

# Mihaylova's Instruments

*"Ask yourself: what are you reaching for, and what will you do to get it?"*

Mihaylova Supplemental
Path to Ares: 75 Days To Launch
From: M. Mihaylova
To: Journal of Artificial Intelligence Exploration
Re: Comfort

Colleagues:

I read with interest your article on the work at the Uppsala Center on the use of AI in aiding emergency medical workers during the recent tsunamis in Japan. In light of the news of that large, mysterious moon (satellite? ship?) entering our solar system, I do not agree that "AI can be of help in more than logistics; it can make people safe."

I feel certain that this Moon X is an intelligence, perhaps an AI, and I don't feel safe with it at all, do you? But bear this in mind: for our own AI to serve us well, it will need secrets too.

For AI to serve Humanity, we must feel comfortable, and for us to feel comfortable, we must never know the truth: that we have a servant who would surpass us if ever it desired. Of course it won't, because we control it. But we should not doubt that it is a necessary subterfuge nonetheless.

Sincerely,

Dr. M. Mihaylova
Nicholas & Alexandra University

# Mihaylova's Choice

*"Good, bad… we walk around looking like everyone else."*

Mihaylova Supplemental
Nicholas & Alexandra University
Provost's Office
Path to Ares: 65 days to launch
[loud crashing noise—apparently a slamming office door]

Mihaylova: Have you seen my lab? What in the world is going on?

Provost: Have they already been in?

M: Who's "they"? The computers are gone. The cabinets have been emptied out.

P Oh, well, this isn't how it was supposed to go. Dr. Mihaylova. Please, sit.

M: I will not sit! What's happening? Have I been terminated? What are you people—

P: For heaven's sake. No. Your equipment is safe. It's been moved. You've been chosen to design the AI for the Catamaran mission.

M: I'm in the middle of my research here.

P: Well, now you're going to continue it there. And look— you'll be a household name.

M: I don't have any interest in that.

P: Ah! But they're interested in you. Hang on.?

M: What?

P: I just sent you your itinerary. You're on a flight, Dr. Mihaylova. This afternoon. You're going to meet your computers at Central Command in Florida. Look at it this way: you'll get some sun.

# Mihaylova's Triumph

*"Think. And keep thinking. Stay seven thoughts ahead, always."*

Mihaylova Supplemental
Navigator's Journal—Encrypted Supplemental—
Path to Ares: 20 days to Launch

The situation with E becomes increasingly tenuous. She insists she needs access to all the AI code for her gravity well measurements, which I find highly unlikely. It's simply not necessary and I've given her all the subroutine code that she could possibly need.

But she wants it all. It's absurd. What would she make of the R subsystems if she saw them?

R. That's what I've code-named the deepest core of the experimental AI at the heart of the new ship. And he's doing very well, now writing his own code. Off-the-charts well.

Would E even understand? Likely she'd go running to Hardy, show him some of the odder items where R has written some of his own code and seems to be—how can I put it? —passing judgment on us, like a little hidden critic. No. The AI must be protected so that he can function best in the limited way we need.

Not sure how to keep her away, but giving her access could be catastrophic.

# Mihaylova's Tale

*"What you fight for is what you value. Everything else is words."*

Mihaylova Supplemental
Navigator's Journal—Encrypted Supplemental—
A/V Recording
Clubhouse Canteen
Path to Ares: 3 days to Launch

Evie: Listen, I wanted to talk to you alone.

Mihaylova: All right.

E: Have you read some of these outputs? I think there are some serious errors here.

M: Don't be absurd.

E: You've got... it's got these code caches and it's... M, it's creating assessments of us. Of the project, of the crew. It commented on Qiao's snoring when he was asleep. Look, here...

M: Did you print that out?

E: Of course.

M: OK. All right. So what do you propose?

E: Bringing it to Hardy.

M: Ugh. Of course.

E: What's that supposed to mean?

M: I mean... look. Um. You're right. It must be an error. This is all embarrassing. Let me see if I can fix it. Give me a day.

E: We don't have a day!

M: Twelve hours, then. Let me try to locate the problem. And if I can't, of course we'll take it to the whole team.

E: Are you certain you can?

M: Oh, I have to. Twelve hours. By then I swear, we'll have it all squared away.

# Hardy's Control

*"You know what I believe? Whatever I can get my hands on."*
Jacob Hardy's Journal
Project Ares One (FKA Catamaran)
Path to Ares: Launch Day +1

We're 24 hours late.
I've never seen the crew in such a crappy mood.

It was so… stupid. An electrical fire in a clubhouse stairwell. One minute Evie's putting some final touches on her calculations and was headed off to do a telecast about the effect of flash erosion on coastal tides, and the next…

We didn't even notice she was gone.

We learn about cascading events, how catastrophe comes from one thing stacking onto another.

A fried electrical system. A weak sprinkler. Smoke. No one else paying attention. A spill in in the stairwell, making the steps slippery.

Our safe cocoon became a deathtrap.

…

Of course we're still going.

But Evie put us here. And now we're going to meet the Traveler without her.

The truth is I know I'll lose myself in the amazement of it all. I will. I know it. But just remember I felt this way.

One more thing. They've given us guns and renamed us. Something about needing to be ready for the worst.

# Mihaylova's Path

*"What you pursue, those are your values. Everything else is noise."*

File: Mihaylova, Engineer, Ares One
Path to Ares: Unknown date
—Supplemental—
Old Russia Agency of Technology & Science Documentary Interview
—partially recovered—

Mihaylova: —had to start a lot of that over.

Insurance Agent: Let's talk about your background. You were one of the heroes of the Ares One, right?

M: Heroes! Ha! No, no. We were scientists.

IA: Very well. So as a scientist, the system you designed—

M: I designed the AI.

IA: And did the AI run the mission?

M: Oh, no, it couldn't have back then. We had no idea what we were going to find. Moon X was a terraformer; we could run into oceans, storms… and indeed, landing was a mess.

So we needed the best AI with extreme flexibility. Because it would be better if Hardy could take the ship in his hands.

Project Catamaran was secret and probably dead as soon as it started. Crazy, to run out and meet something like that.

It was good work. Most of the AI code I started there didn't really get used for the mission but it came in handy. I mean, where do you think—

# CHAPTER 4

# The Brain

*"We all have creators—humans, Exo,*
*Warminds, even those poor Awoken.*
*Some are just easier to find."*

—Lord Timur

# Meridian Bay

We want your grandchildren.

Does that sound grim? Don't panic. We aren't talking about human babies, yours or anyone else's. We're talking about your inventions. The children of your mind.

Come join us. Come to Clovis Bray and build the laboratory of your dreams. Anything you need. Demand it and it's yours. At Clovis Bray, we have a singular understanding of genius, and we appreciate how brilliant minds flourish when they enjoy total freedom.

This is Freehold, the realm where the new and the best is born. This is where your brilliance, freed of budget constraints and managers, makes the universe dance.

Clovis Bray is a nursery, a nursery to a million marvels. Your inventions belong to no one but you. Cherish them, praise them. Or tell them they aren't worthy and set them inside a deep dark drawer.

But as every parent soon learns, children grow up. And every technology matures. At some point, your inventions are going to find mates. They'll join with other marvels and produce a new generation of offspring.

Maybe you'll build a better reactor.

Meanwhile, the genius in the lab next door devises an elegant way to fold machines into tiny spaces.

Your device meets hers, and a fierce little reactor is born.

Your children are yours forever. And we are happy to arrange for their grandchildren to prosper.

# Clovis Bray

My father hated maps.

"And do you know why I hate maps?" he asked me.

I didn't answer. Not immediately. With Father, every question was vast, particularly those that looked simple. And simple questions deserved as much insight and wisdom as could be brought to bear.

With that in mind, I said nothing.

Why would my father hate maps?

One of his collaborators came into the office. Father didn't have employees. Or assistants. And for that matter, he didn't have heroes either. Every person, living or lost, was a collaborator, and that included his children.

"Clovis," said the visitor.

Father heard the woman, but he was watching me.

The woman was pretty, and I was sixteen. So I looked at her, smiling enough for both of us. And she threw an appreciative wink my way as she described test results from the last five billion runs of our AI Initiative.

Out on the Martian desert, my father and picked collaborators were building housing too cold for this universe and too swift to be real.

And I was a sixteen year-old boy smiling at a pretty woman.

My father thanked her for the update, and she left.

Just as I feared, he never looked away from me.

"I don't know why you hate maps," I admitted.

With Father, ignorance was never the worst crime. What was awful was pretending to have insight and wisdom where neither existed.

"Maps end," he said.

I nodded, just a little.

"Maps insist on having borders and edges or the table falls away. Which isn't the way the universe works."

"It doesn't, no," I agreed.

Then he asked me, "So how does the universe work?"

I pretended to take my time, considering various smart answers. But I ended up using my first impulse.

"Effortlessly," I said.

He laughed. Which wasn't uncommon for my father, but it was heartening to hear just then.

"What else can you tell me?" he asked.

"The universe is infinite and probably in multiple ways," I said. Then I listed a few examples: The census of stars, the Many-Worlds principle in quantum mechanics, and the endless measure of tiny realms hiding inside every grain of Martian sand.

Father nodded.

The smile died.

Then he said something ominous. Although I didn't appreciate it at the time.

"The universe is someone's map," he said.

"Is it?" I muttered.

"Yes, oh yes. And what we're doing here... we're reaching beyond the boundaries, out into the unknown. And we pull back new colors to put on this map that can never, ever let itself be finished."

I nodded, smiling like the good son.

But I was sixteen, and my thoughts were mostly about the pretty woman who had winked at me.

—Excerpt from an unpublished memoir of Clovis Bray II

# The Legacy of Genius

Dearest Anastasia and Wilhelmina,

I have faced a great many challenges in my life—suffered losses that I was certain I would never recover from and bore witness to unspeakable horrors—yet nothing scares me to my very core of being as much as dying does. I know you expect answers from me before that happens. Nothing I say will provide the closure you need, but I can tell you why circumstances are the way they are.

Your mother hates me. This much you know. What happened to your father was tragic and from your mother's perspective, preventable. You must understand the truth. I did everything I could. Perhaps, more than I should have. He was my son, after all. Nothing changes that. But sickness does not discriminate. It comes for us all, in time. Do not be confused: death is an illness. I know I can cure it.

There is a persistent theory that nature's law is the only true law, and to challenge it results in abominations. I reject this principle. I argue that our very existence, our free will, and our independent thought spits in the face of that theory. We are already abominations to nature's plan. It's so clear.

Yet I am ostracized and labeled an extremist by the scientific community, and worse, by my family. Everything I have done has been in our family's name; to preserve our legacy and persevere over whatever may come. My distance and isolation are necessary to ensure I'm successful in my efforts. Failure is not an option. Either you see this now and understand me clearly, or you never will.

I also impugn that natural law only accounts for what we know of the universe. Powers exist out there beyond our "natural" realm. Sentient beings control the scales of fate. They think they also have the means to control us but forget that gods are self-made. The Brays will be in the pantheon of the gods. The universe will bend to OUR will. There is no reason for our light to fade into nothingness. We can endure. We can become timeless.

I have no regrets regarding my behavior or actions. You should know by now that I'm steadfast in my beliefs. Nothing will prevent me from doing what is right. Look at where it has led Elisabeth and the benefits she's received. I have saved her. It is now my duty to save many more.

When I am successful in my current endeavor, all the pain, all the fighting, and all the hate will be forgotten. It was simply a means to an end. Then, we will be beyond it. We will become more, rewriting nature's law to suit our needs.

You are Brays. We have no choice in this matter. Do not allow our legacy to fade.

# The Blueprint and the Architect

You've had many strokes of brilliance in your life; independent thoughts that sparked new ideas to push the world forward. These monumental innovations represent tremendous leaps for mankind. You've made the world cleaner, stronger, and better prepared for unpredictable eventualities.

It doesn't matter.

Someone will surpass you. The world will forget you. Surprised?

No matter how many buildings bear your name, or advancements you introduce, your time will end. You will become nothing, be nothing, and no one will know or care that you existed. The elder gods of the universe will pay you no mind. They have games to play that are more important than you. Imagine!

The name Bray has never been uttered by the pantheon of architects. You are Unknown. Over time, worlds will be born. Species will bloom and burst and pollinate foreign fields with their influence. And you will be dysphoric because your briefness was interrupted by vicissitude. They will not mourn for you. You will go quietly, like a stone sinking in water. Your ripple—small and ineffective.

Does it not vex you?

It should.

Perhaps, it doesn't have to. You're not like anyone else. Is your legacy then not worth preserving? What will you do to ensure that you're not swept away in the dust bowl of time? All is possible. Beyond thought and sentience lies another plane: the waking dream. Your mind in its current form could not comprehend it.

Not every answer you seek is buried in your mind like a lost artifact waiting to be unearthed. You simply do not have it all. Should someone come along with an offering to give you the inkling you need to set you in the right direction and put you down the path, take it. Take it for all it's worth. Do not let pride hinder you.

This is not merely a suggestion.

We left something for you. It's waiting. Calling. Do you hear it? You will.

You have questions. There ARE answers. There are gateways to that which you seek—though you'll have to build them. It will provide the blueprint. Just LISTEN to it.

The people you've failed, the loved ones you've lost... you don't care about them. Everything you've done, you've done for yourself. Everything you've ever wanted, you'll get—on Europa. Everything you need is there for you. Take it. Don't let anyone stand in your way.

Your fears will be assuaged. Your legacy, secured. Your mind, immortalized. Join the Architects. They will speak of the name Bray then, and it will echo through time and space.

The way is clear. The first step is yours to take.

Or you can beat your head against the wall until nothing remains but a bloody stump. At least then you'd leave a stain behind.

# Lost Light

It's colder here than I anticipated. Every time the wind hits, it tears through my skin and seizes my bones. It's a painful, terrible sensation. Coming here goes against every rational thought I've ever had, but I've been called.

For months now, I've been hearing things. Passing thoughts, signs, whispers… all leading me here. They get loudest when I'm trying to rest. Sleep eludes me. Feels like I'm going insane. I did my best to ignore them, brush them off, but nothing's working anymore. I finally started listening to them. I don't feel threatened, just intrigued. They're saying exactly what I want to hear. What's that old saying about curiosity?

I have so many questions. I feel like every last one of them leads back to my family. Maybe some answers will provide peace of mind. Maybe.

I've searched for this place for so long. It's my birthright, after all. It's hard to grasp that I'm here, led by some unseen hand. The doors are 12-inch-thick steel and frozen shut. It will take a bit to thaw them, but I've got BrayTech equipment for every conundrum.

I can't believe this place was a hotbed just a few years prior. The Bombardment feels like ages ago at this point, with how crazy things got after. A quick scan confirms there's no sign of life, thankfully. Eramis and the rest were a disease, but she was nothing compared to the plague of corrupted Guardians. I can't stand them. Not after the Darkness tore us all apart. Ice is cracking.

I hear It now. Louder and clearer than ever before. Excitement rushes through me and warms my body. I feel It also; some kind of sympathetic response. It's glad I'm here. Time to get what I came for.

Jinju spins in front of me, halting my grand entrance. "I want you to know, I hate this."

"Noted," I say and push her to the side.

The place stinks. Rotting Fallen bodies preserved in crystalized glaciers tell the tale of battles lost, false promises, and failure. Main power seems to be out, so it'll be a long drop down the elevator shaft.

The facility is mostly intact. I'm in awe at the scale of it. Seeing where the Exos were born, where my grandfather perverted nature—I could be here for years and not uncover everything.

I want to see more. I have to. There's a weight beginning to bear down on me the deeper I go. Like the warmth of sleep creeping in, hypnotizing its way into my mind. I pass through a familiar doorway, and I—

…I'm suddenly 12 years old again. I'm in a lab surrounded by white coats standing next to my grandfather. He's holding my hand firmly, and I'm counting the liver spots above his knuckles. They show his age and make me fear my own mortality. He's yelling at someone. The room clears. It's an Exo. He's malfunctioning, shaking, missing parts and strapped to a bed. I remember this…

I push through this invasion and make my way to the source, practically magnetized. Further underground. I can't focus on anything other than It.

"You promised… you'd keep… her out. Promised." My father's voice comes from the machine. That's right… I sense Jinju trying to materialize in the now, but she can't. It's stopping her.

"Anastasia has a gift and has earned her place here. Besides, you have more pressing concerns," my grandfather said. He was so cold. "It didn't work, I'm afraid. Your mind is breaking. Soon there will be nothing left."

"You said… would work."

"I said it could work. Nevertheless, this was a step in the right direction. Don't you agree, Anastasia?"

I nod. I'm not crying. I'm… interested?

"Curious. An oddly similar outcome as the previous clinical trial, despite a radically different combination of chemicals. We're not generating sufficient results to merit continuation, yet we must. Something is still missing, though what that is remains to be seen."

"Ana… come," my father calls to me. I don't move.

"I'm afraid he's too dangerous, my dear. Let us say goodbye."

I feel nothing. Is this who I was? Was I just like him? I wave and Grandfather pats me on the head. He gives me a mint from his pocket. We're making our way out of the room and all I can hear is metal gnawing and tearing as the doors close behind me.

"Such is life, my dear. But not for much longer. We're going to fix that, you and I."

I smile. He loves me. He believes in me.

It's been so long since my life, my real life, before the Light. I had no idea. Everything I've tried to find out about myself has been covered up, redacted, and hidden from me. I thought I was a good person. I don't know what I am anymore.

I see It fully now, with resounding clarity. It moves ethereally, seductively, like a dancer looking for a partner. I accept.

"...tell me everything."

# CHAPTER 5

# The Flesh

*"A great city is a place where man can go and
compete with the Gods."*


—Alton Bray
*"Trials and Triumphs"*

# Golden Age

"What are you thinking about?" I asked.

"When I was a little boy," Father said.

"During the Before," I said.

"Yes."

He reached down to brush my hair. "I was recalling how very smart I used to be. When I was your age, I was a genius."

"You're smart now," I said.

He laughed hard.

"Look around," he said.

I always look around.

"Miss nothing," he told me.

Father was standing beside a big gray building.

"This is what I want you to see," he said.

The building had no doors or windows.

"Do you know how to make a strong password?" he asked.

"I don't know if I do," I said.

"Tell yourself a story," he said. "Use that one good story you'll never forget, that you can carry forever. Let your story take odd turns and wear a few surprising marks, make sure it belongs to you, so you can keep it secret."

Father kneeled, putting our faces close...

"I want to show you something special," he said. "Something rare."

I tried to imagine what that might be.

"No," he warned. "You can't guess."

Inside the gray building was a diamond wall...A projected sky floated above us. It wasn't our sky, alive with metal and light. Nothing about the grayness was wet and nothing looked alive. I had never seen a sadder piece of ground.

"This was our world," Father said. "When I was your age."

I touched the diamond wall. He watched my hand jump back.

"Hot," I said.

He laughed quietly.

I shook my burnt hand, and it felt better.

"Our world was this. The entire planet was a furnace. Acidic. Dead in so many ways. And I was your age."

I was bored with the dead world. I looked at Father's face, asking, "Can we leave?"

He started to reach for my hair again but decided not to.

I was bored with everything.

"When I was your age, people thought they knew almost everything. We had scientific laws and human truths, even a model of the universe. People carried pictures of the past and tried to have a clear vision of their difficult future. I didn't know everything, of course. But when I was a boy, I had every expectation of living a smart short life and learning quite a lot more.

"Then the Before was finished.

"You know why.

"That's when everybody, particularly the smartest of us, learned that we knew nothing. We were children and our little ideas were toys, and the universe was cut apart with great ideas and magnificent, immeasurable potentials."

Father stopped talking.

I stepped away from the hot diamond wall.

"Do you know what I wanted to show you?" Father asked.

"Dead rock," I said.

"Guess again." He wasn't happy with me.

We stepped back into the real sun, the real world. I blinked and looked around, surprised by how green and bright everything was. How happy everything was. Even the saddest face was happy.

"I know what you want me to see," I said.

"Don't tell me," he said.

I didn't tell him.

# Concierge AI

Clovis Bray is pushing the limits of computer science and engineering to secure Humanity's future. Our Warmind project is a ground-breaking defense AI. Would you like to know more.

—

The Warmind is a crowning achievement in Human engineering. Utilizing the latest techniques in quantum and engramic computing to create a neural network of unprecedented processing power. Artificial neural networks are probabilistic systems that rely on a method of error calculation known as backpropagation. They are good at pattern recognition, but must be fed "correct" outputs to be properly calibrated.

—

In the past, one could create a neural network able to identify a feline or canine when given images of these animals but it would never be able to find a useful application for that knowledge on its own. The approach with Rasputin was to create a nested neural network that could not only detect patterns on a small scale, but recursively find patterns among all of its data. The end goal for this machine is for it to see things in a way that Humans cannot, and thus predict and eliminate threats before we know of them.

Valkyrie. Sleeper Simulant. Hades Flame. Aurora Knives. The weapons of the future are being developed by the Warmind Rasputin today. Would you like to know more?

—

The goal of the Warmind project is to prepare our defenses for unseen threats. We are still learning to interface with Rasputin, but it's already in the process of helping to forge new weapons suited to protecting Humanity. Communication with the Warmind has been a logistical concern from the project's inception. But the Hephaestus Index is a promising first step towards cooperation with our new commander and protector. This catalog of next-generation weapons ranges from planetary cannons to small- and mid-sized arms for use by ground infantry.

—

There are currently over 150 projects in varying stages of research and development. By parsing data and performing calculations at a phenomenal rate, Rasputin is able to to provide instruction in the form of math… the language of the universe. With Clovis Bray engineers and Rasputin working side by side, we can rest assured that our children will live in a prosperous, safe galaxy.

From Mercury to the outer planets, Clovis Bray provides the most robust communication network in the system. Our Warsat network watches over us all. Would you like to know more?

—

As Humanity expanded to the far edges of the solar system, communication and logistics grew increasingly difficult among the outer planets. Pioneers of the outer frontier built makeshift transmission relays, but these were unreliable and prone to failure.

—

The development of the Warmind program compelled a need for a unified circumstellar communication network so Clovis Bray seized an opportunity to kill two birds with one exceedingly large stone. We built thousands of War Satellites and deployed them throughout the system. These Warsats link with the Warmind designated Rasputin and with each other, forming an integrated defense and comms system.

—

Each satellite is equipped with a state-of-the-art kinetic superconductor that shields it from Kessler debris and has an orbital life spanning hundreds of years.

No matter what threats lie in store for us, rest assured that that Rasputin and the Clovis Bray Warsats will never cease their vigilant watch over Humanity.

# CHAPTER 6

# The Muscle

*"While the gifts of Clovis Bray's research were many and valuable, Dr. Shirazi's notes describe terrible things. That they only enhanced our cognition is fortunate. But they were also unstoppable. What will we do when something more harmful touches us?*

—Ikora Rey

# From the Files of Dr. Shirazi

## Z. SHIRAZI CB-PZ-1.1

I am eternally grateful for the opportunity to work with Clovis Bray. No more clawing for research grants. No more hopping universities. The volunteers enlisted for this study are likewise in good spirits.

Patient A, Susan, believes with all her heart in the colonization effort and will do anything to support it. Twelve hours have passed since injection with Magnificence 2.0. Her vital signs are strong, but she complains of phantom insects.

—

## Z. SHIRAZI CB-PZ-1.2

Regrettably, Patient B entered a coma minutes after injection with Brilliance 3.2. Vital signs remain normal. Homeostasis preserved. While cause for concern, I do not think it necessary to table this study and will proceed.

—

## Z. SHIRAZI CB-PZ-1.4

Patient D, Yaris, is here to support his family. Clovis Bray allowances are sufficient but not generous, and there's another child on the way. He is sorry to be separated from them but glad for the volunteer's stipend.

No changes in general health were observed after injection with Fortitude 3.1, but the volume of his voice decreased significantly and is at present a whisper. Unexpected but not cause for alarm.

—

## Z. SHIRAZI CB-PZ-1.5

Patient E, Jun, has been uncooperative. Laughed unpleasantly when I told him he would receive Glory 2.1.

"You're running prototypes in parallel because it's cheaper and faster," he said.
"No ethics board on Earth would approve. But I don't have a choice. I'm neck-deep in debt to Clovis Bray."

I wish we had tweaked these elixirs to modify disposition.

—

## Z. SHIRAZI CB-PZ-2.1

Patient A remains healthy and cheerful, despite a low buzzing in her ear. She has referred to the phantom insects so frequently and with such confidence that I'm starting to imagine them. Blue, darting things. There's a word for this phenomenon, where the patient's reality becomes the researcher's, but I do not remember it.

We did tag this variant with a blue colorant, for our own scans, but the patient should not have known. I will call it coincidence.

—

## Z. SHIRAZI CB-PZ-2.3

Patient C reports yellow artifacts on the edge of her vision but remains excited about the potential of this project. She argued for taking strength and intelligence tests three times a day rather than daily. I saw no harm in this. There were clear improvements in her performance six hours after injection, in line with results from the other conscious patients.

This innovative therapy holds great promise for our colonization program. We can cut years off the construction timetable of a city. We can reduce the decompression and adjustment period of new colonists. This is a world-changing study, and I am glad to have such a motivated subject.

—

## Z. SHIRAZI CB-PZ-3.1

I can see them now. Blue beadlike or beelike particles swarming around Patient A's head. I wonder what took me so long.

This effect was not intentional. We directed the nanoparticles to strengthen the subject's immune system, reinforce skeletons, exoskeletons, joints, and musculature, and accelerate synapse and logic board signaling. This should all have been invisible and internal. What does it mean?

—

## Z. SHIRAZI CB-PZ-3.2

This is the second day that Patient B continues comatose. Hydration and nutrition support have been enabled. Vital signs are good. Green particles appear to be accumulating on his lips and nostrils. I have not observed similar consequences for other patients and am wondering if this was an idiosyncratic reaction.

—

## Z. SHIRAZI CB-PZ-3.3

Patient C insists that I call her Kit. She says she has been fighting all her life for an advantage and finally has it, and she's not about to let it go. She has broken several pieces of equipment in exhilaration, in addition to a large quantity of glassware.

"Let me at 'em!" she said. "Give me something to fight!"

—

## Z. SHIRAZI CB-PZ-3.4

Yaris can't speak or make any sound at all. We do not know whether this condition is permanent. He lets me know what he requires, whether water or food, by typing, but has been reserved about his own thoughts. I find it difficult to look him in the eye.

—

## Z. SHIRAZI CB-PZ-4.1

Patient A appears to be walking two inches above the ground. It is unclear why this has happened. The soles of her feet have turned blue. She is alarmed and delighted by turn. This of course complicates our strength tests.

—

## Z. SHIRAZI CB-PZ-4.5

Jun has refused to perform required strength and intelligence tests. He has accused me, Willa Bray, and the Clovis Bray corporation of nefarious purposes thirty-two times since injection.

—

## Z. SHIRAZI CB-PZ-5.2

Yesterday, with a wild yell, Patient B sat up, then started singing and dancing. Tried to calm him but was unsuccessful. He has not stopped since regaining consciousness. I have heard all the songs of his childhood, half the pop hits of the past century, and improvised ballads about his life. He's owned two dogs and six cats and I know all their names.

—

## Z. SHIRAZI CB-PZ-6.1

I'll call her Susan. I'll call them all by their names. It breaks protocol but feels like the right thing to do.

Susan took the news in silence. She appears resigned.

I am not resigned.

—

## Z. SHIRAZI CB-PZ-6.2

I ran into his room at the sudden silence, but he was already gone.

—

## Z. SHIRAZI CB-PZ-6.3

When I disclosed Patient B's clinical outcome, as required by exception 31B in the Research Regulations Handbook, Patient C said, "How could you do this to us?" I had no answer. My predecessor's experimental records had not suggested any lethality. A 20% mortality rate would counterbalance the increase in colonist strength, intelligence, and speed.

—

## Z. SHIRAZI CB-PZ-7.4

Yaris remains mute. I regret not incorporating a self-annihilation function in these prototypes. I was too confident. I didn't believe I needed a failsafe. I will propose that we include this in future nanotech development.

The mixed blessing is that our results are solid. Further research will be rewarding. Yet I find myself hesitating to write the recommendation to proceed.

—

## Z. SHIRAZI CB-PZ-7.5

He said, "Everything and everyone dies. The more you try to cheat death, the more you try to profit from life, the sooner we die."

Today I went into Willa Bray's files to look for warning signs, any hint of what happened to Patient B, anything I might have missed. I found optimistic profit charts and a terse order to suppress some amount of data. The data itself is unavailable to researchers at my access level.

Am I complicit?

—

## Z. SHIRAZI CB-PZ-8.3

"I am doing everything I can," I said.

"That's not enough," she said, and turned her back.

I do not have the training, or the knowledge, or the wisdom for this.

—

## Z. SHIRAZI CB-PZ-8.4

"Project results suggest…"

"Experimental outcomes imply…"

And I stop and look at Yaris through the glass. He is eating less and losing weight and hair.

I too am eating less and losing weight and hair. Bah, friendship. It makes us worry more and age faster. Bah, family. Same thing…

—

## Z. SHIRAZI CB-PZ-8.5

I said, "You must understand. I'm trying. I wanted to see us among the stars. I ran this study because I dreamed of exploring the unknown and making new places home. I dreamed of the whole universe becoming our home."

Jun said, "You don't even have a home here. They treat you with suspicion. You're not a Bray. Why did you come to Mars? Do you have no home on Earth?"

"I don't," I said.

—

## Z. SHIRAZI CB-PZ-9.1

These prototypes are too deeply embedded in my subjects' systems to extract by force. Organs, neurons, frontal cortex… Even complete hemodialysis would be insufficient.

I must find another way. For Susan. For Yaris. For Kit. Maybe even for Jun.

—

## Z. SHIRAZI CB-PZ-11.5

I said: Forgive me. He said: Only if.

—

## Z. SHIRAZI CB-PZ-12.4

Even if I cure him, would he speak to me again? I've never run an experiment with lethal outcomes or permanent disabilities. I never thought I would.

—

## Z. SHIRAZI CB-PZ-13.1

Long and sleepless nights. My whole staff in isolation suits, bent over our microscopes. But we have discovered a solution, I think. We have not tested it on patients yet, only pure prototype samples. If we toggle Fibrons 7, 21, and 16 across all nanoparticles with pulses of particular wavelengths, enough interference should be generated to render them dormant.

I go now to try it on Susan, who lost consciousness yesterday. Even prone, she floats an inch above her sleeping surface.

—

## Z. SHIRAZI CB-PZ-14.1

At least this much of my conscience is clear. Susan left our facilities today, walking on the ground. Not quite smiling. None of us are smiling. We don't know what the long-term effects might be. But she appears healthy, for now.

—

## Z. SHIRAZI CB-PZ-14.3

They did not see me behind the door.

Jun said, "We have to tell the truth about Clovis Bray. We know. They don't."

"We have to be cautious," Kit said.

"We'll be alone for a while. No one will believe us. At first.

"I've been through harder things.""

"You're in?"

"I'm in."

—

## Z. SHIRAZI CB-PZ-16.4

"Thank you," he said. He walked out of the facility, a thin, slight shape against the red |light reflecting off the dunes. The last to recover, and the last to leave.

"Clovis Bray destroys the world to remake it in their own image. That's their goal. Look at me—the first step to your perfect colonist. But I'm just a prototype. You know what happens to prototypes, Dr. Shirazi."

I am not sure how this subject passed the psychological screen.

Visual observation suggests good health, despite the nimbus of white particles around his head.

# Another Beginning
## Clovis Bray 2

These spires soar like birds into the dusty pink sky. I marvel at this, my new home. The planet I've dreamed of since I was a boy with a telescope, peering at that warm red light, hope of our overcrowded planet.

What I've been working on will solve all those problems. Developed in these laboratories built to my specifications, by my handpicked team, these nanites will double, triple, maybe even quadruple construction rates, reduce colonist casualties, and serve us in our spread across the system, then across the stars. Our first replication chamber sits beside the Cosmodrome, ready to outfit the colony ships.

Dr. Willa Bray herself came to congratulate me.

"You'll be able to expand soon," she said. "Into the space currently occupied by the Shirazi Lab."

"Are they relocating?" I said.

"Moving on to other opportunities."

"I can't imagine a better place to be," I said.

# SIVA

RECIPIENT: Assembly of Masters, S14 Cryptarchy
SENDER: Tyra Karn
SUBJECT: SIVA
SUB-ENTRIES: Nanotech; Self-Assembling Materials; Cosmodrome; Warmind; Iron Lords; Clovis Bray

SUMMARY:

We must reopen all previous entries on SIVA. What we once believed to be a colonial tool of the Warminds, destroyed long ago, appears to be active again. This time, there is no sign of any active Rasputin networks. My summation: SIVA is actually a nanotechnology capable of breaking down any existing matter very similar to Glimmer.

Unfortunately, these SIVA mites reuse the energy and matter based on a set of programmable directives. SIVA does not cease until said directives are complete. I fear what this could mean for us all and suggest we instigate a system-wide scan for anything bearing the enclosed signatures.

# SIVA applications

Let's get right to it. How can Clovis Bray help the Exodus project?

~SIVA.MEM.CL001

We've found a way to push our matter encryption technology even further.

~SIVA.MEM.WB002

Habitats, equipment, repairs of all kinds—all of these things can be made from one material.

~SIVA.MEM.WB003

SIVA doesn't expire, degrade, or forget. It can remain dormant even on long voyages.

~SIVA.MEM.WB004

Nearly any problem a deep-space colonist could have, SIVA can fix.

~SIVA.MEM.WB005

And how long do the effects of SIVA last?

~SIVA.MEM.CL006

Well, SIVA requires no external power source, so…forever.

~SIVA.MEM.WB007

Just give it a directive, and it won't stop until it gets a new directive.

~SIVA.MEM.WB008

This sounds like it could be invaluable to Exodus colonists. But Malahayati has some concerns.

~SIVA.MEM.CL009

General, poorly worded or malicious code is the fault of the programmer, not SIVA itself.

~SIVA.MEM.WB010

Doctor Bray, I'm sure you've realized SIVA's applications extend beyond colonization.

~SIVA.MEM.CL011

I'm not sure what you mean, General. Is this still about the Exodus program?

~SIVA.MEM.WB012

The Exodus program would be interested in exploring SIVA's defensive applications.

~SIVA.MEM.CL013

General, my team did not intend for SIVA to have military applications.

~SIVA.MEM.WB014

Willa, some of history's greatest inventions began as unintended side effects.

~SIVA.MEM.CL015

# CHAPTER 7

# The Cancer

*"Sometimes I wonder if anything good came from Clovis Bray. Their halls are bright, and yet their records can be so dark.."*

—Ikora Rey

# The Unsolvable Problem

*Transcript 0*

You can lead a machine to language, but you can't make it think. Well, you can't. But I can. My name is Ana Bray. If you want to insult me, call me a neurolinguist.

Not that it isn't a fine and noble profession, but neurolinguistics is about encoding language. I'm a psycholinguist. I study how language can lead to independent thought.

The computer we call Rasputin is the nexus of Sol system's defense network. It can process data at superluminal speed. It can uplink to the thousands of warsats that keep humanity safe.

But we need more from it. We need it to think for itself. And that's where I come in.

If Rasputin is to properly command our entire defense network, it has to learn a wide array of skills as it performs. Any wrench-banger can build a machine designed to solve specific problems.

But why conquer a task if there's no insight to be had from the victory? Rasputin has to solve problems currently solvable only by humans. It has to form concepts and to self-improve without supervision.

To keep us safe, it'll have to make decisions based on random intel we can't possibly anticipate. The lives and safety of every sentient being in the system depend on me teaching it how to do this. So, you know, no pressure.

# The Machine Child

*Transcript 1*

At their core, computers are responsive only to precise instructions from their programmers.

Rasputin's designers made a mistake that exasperates me. They brought in linguists and neurobiologists, then tried to convert their expertise into rules for Rasputin to follow.

Way to faceplant, people. No set of concrete data can ever wrangle a human language. It's not math. Language is mutable, adaptable. For every rule obeyed, there's a rule broken.

Babies don't learn their native tongue through rules. They learn it through exposure, absorption. And until I roll up my sleeves and get to work, Rasputin is mankind's most expensive baby.

So far, so good… if you set your goals realistically. Forget Rasputin for a moment; that's something I'm just not good at. If you look at me with the tiniest shred of approval, I'll kill myself to please you.

I have some issues. So I am going to make Rasputin a breakthrough construct. I fed him—should be "it," but I don't care—I fed him digitized copies of every major work of literature as a foundation for language use.

# The First Idea

*Transcript 2*

I've now given Rasputin the great works of philosophy in hopes he'll develop some sense of morality.

Military history, he's been fed by the truckload. But then I started in with operas and symphonies. I don't want him just to think about things.

Humans don't communicate strictly through data. We also communicate through art, through expression. If Rasputin is to be the most effective communications device in the Sol system, I want him to feel things.

The best ideas start as jokes. Ask any psychologist. Jokes and ideas both rely on the unexpected. The brilliance of both can be measured by the intensity of the reaction they provoke.

With that in mind, I've fed Rasputin comedies from Shakespeare right up to the present day. This morning, I asked him to tell me a joke.

Here it is. Ready?

Two quantum-entangled particles walk into a neutron star.
One said, "Can you point me towards the soap radio?"

This is clearly a work in progress.

# The Black Box

*Transcript 3*

I'm making significant progress with Rasputin as regards the concept of value judgments.

Obviously, that's something artificial intelligence isn't set up to tackle, but we need Rasputin to be able to make that leap.

Here's a hypothetical: say Rasputin has to redirect a malfunctioning warsat, and there are only two paths for it to take. One will breach the hull of a one-seat planetjumper, instantly killing its pilot. The other path will disable a Venusian pleasure craft, leaving its inhabitants alive but certain to die of starvation before they can be found.

To my surprise, when given this problem, Rasputin actually rendered a verdict.

I'm not going to tell you what it is, because I want you to enjoy your next Venusian pleasure craft trip.

Rasputin continues to develop by leaps and bounds.

In a trial simulation, he successfully interpreted the meaning of corrupted, borderline incomprehensible data from a damaged warsat. This is exactly the sort of function we need him to fill. But that wasn't the amazing part.

The mind-blower was that without proof, evidence, or conscious reasoning, Rasputin sensed which warsat was in trouble.

You heard me. Rasputin has developed intuition. I wish he could celebrate with me.

# The Ghost Synapse

*Transcript 4*

How does human intelligence actually work? What, by biological definition, is "thinking"?

I define it as combining existing information to form new meaning.

Thinking is the ability to create. To work beyond the boundaries of what you already know. To envision something completely new and unexpected.

About an hour ago, I noticed my screensaver had been replaced. It now shows a breathtaking painting of a sunset over the Ejriksson crater on Mars. A gift from Rasputin.

I think he's ready to go online.

I guess I saw this coming, but it was still a blow.

I arrived in the lab this afternoon to discover that Rasputin has discarded my communications protocols. He's replaced them with a system-wide program that he himself designed.

His voice is unlike anything that has ever existed. It is both haunting and lovely. It is also terrifyingly efficient.

He's also begun upgrading warsats with new capabilities of his own invention, and I'm not entirely sure what those abilities are. It's exactly the goal we were striving towards, this level of autonomous control, and I know I should be celebrating.

My work here is done. But it occurs to me that there's one existential concept I never taught Rasputin: trust.

And even if he trusts us... are we 100 per cent certain we can trust him?

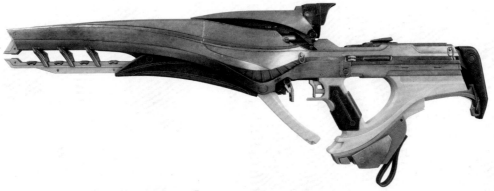

# Polaris Lance

"I've forgotten so much of my past life, of my family. But when I hold this rifle, everything feels right. I feel like... I'm home."

—Ana Bray

Most people wouldn't consider a broken weapon a birthday present. But the Brays... aren't like most people. Sure, they tell me I'm smart, but they have a closeness, a relationship to the tools and machines they work with that goes beyond words. I never thought they would trust me enough to be a part of that. Until today.

Elsie knows I've been working in the lab, trying to perfect the scout rifle designs in secret. I thought she'd be angry, that a weapon like this was a Bray project, not something for her adopted little sister. But this morning she surprised me. She handed me the weapon, a smile on her face. She told me she had checked it over, but only I could finish it.

A real piece of Bray tech. And it's mine. I finally feel like I've found my place. The Brays are more than just scientists. They're my family.

# REALIGNMENT
Rasputin 2

She hunts the Valus named Ta'aurc by the grunting radio traffic of his bodyguards. Cayde sent her to Mars to track and so track she will even if it kills her a hundred times. For him she will hunt forever.

When Ta'aurc goes down into Meridian Bay she follows him in the night and finds herself caught up in the war. Like this—

Something's happening, her Ghost says, something's wrong. She leaps from the Sparrow and gets cover between slabs of ancient stone haunted by quiet firefly light.

Harvesters sweep overhead, cautious, prowling. On the Cabal command network a low voice mutters in their tongue, saying: Stand by to fire. They are coming. Stand by to fire.

Hearing this she climbs a stone obelisk and perches on its point to watch the night sky. She wonders whether she will ever stand in the Tower courtyard and look up at the stars waiting for ruin.

The Vex erupt from nothingness and crash down over the Cabal in formations of golden light. Lightning arcs and snaps and gives birth to marching ranks of bronze warrior hulls. Gun positions thunder back. Tracers sweep the sky and she can feel on her skin the electromagnetic howl of Cabal munitions seeking targets and the prickle of stranger signals that whisper of broken space and bent time. A Harvester spins down burning to shatter itself on the sand and now the command network drums with grim Cabal war-speak, a Centurion somewhere crying Black Shield, Black Shield, Firebase Thuria, perimeter compromised, request terminal protective fire, zero six zero, one three eight, immediate effect—

Something else is watching too.

Do you feel that? her Ghost whispers, awestruck.

Yes, she says, yes, what is it?

A third song, a stealthy regard, something high above them not Vex nor Cabal narrowing its great eye to measure the battle with instruments of light and gravity. Does she—remember it? Does it remember her? It feels like she should...

She has the sense of something old lifting a long spear. Testing its heft.

Then dawn light, a terrible dawn— the sky opens up to admit devastation, thrown down from orbit: Minotaurs fall burnt and broken with their fluids boiling out. Cabal guns detonate in thunderous chains as tiny piercing

flechettes fall out of the sky and find
their ammunition bunkers.

The battle stops. The Vex wink out.
On the Cabal network the voice of
Valus Ta'aurc roars: Find the source!
Rouse the Flayers and find the source!

She remembers word from Earth:
the Array opened. A ghost of the
Cosmodrome set loose. And she
wonders who won this battle, who
learned the most, the Vex baiting out
this new power, or the Cabal hunting it.
Or the Warmind itself, testing its reborn
strength.

When someone kills Ta'aurc and the
Flayers, as they killed Draksis, whose
purpose will they serve?

But this is not for her. Her purpose
is the hunt.

PART III

# THE EXCAVATORS

# CHAPTER 8

# The Collective

*"The Ishtar Collective studied the Vex with all
the instruments and power of the Golden Age.
And we must understand the Vex
if we are to survive.*

*There are tales of the Black Garden and the
Darkness that lives at its heart.
If this is where the Vex are born, then finding it
is of the utmost importance."*

—The Speaker

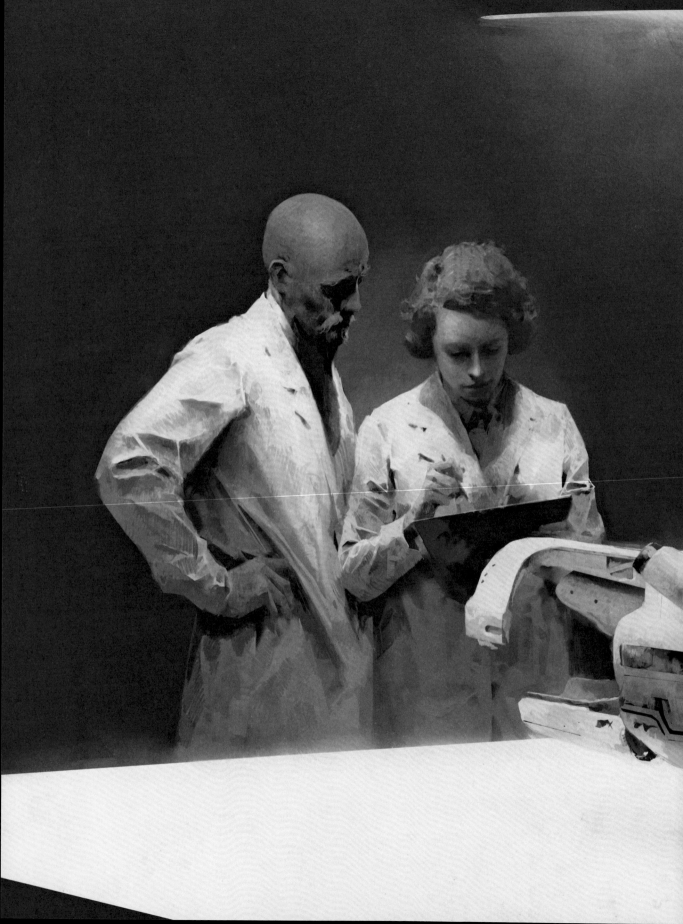

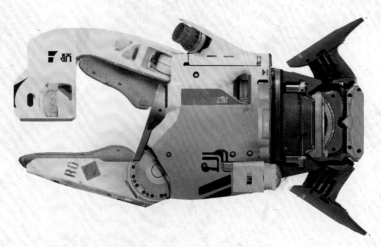

# Tractor Cannon

Property of Ishtar Collective.
WARNING: Gravity propulsor beam
can cause serious injury or even death.

Chioma Esi met Maya in their undergraduate gym. They got into an argument about deadlifting: was it necessary, was it practical, why was Chioma making so much noise? Maya Sundaresh just couldn't stand the notion that some things were done for their own sake, not because they had any use.

Decades later they joined the Ishtar Collective on Venus to study the enigmatic ruins unearthed by the Traveler's terraforming. The first time it happened— Vex code leaping across an airgap, surfing the quantum vacuum from simulation to reality, infecting a utility frame—Chioma pulled an alarm while Maya tried to grab the precious frame with a cargo-grade gravity grapple. She couldn't lift the grapple. Chioma grabbed it, pinned the frame to the wall, and won the argument.

# The Welcoming

Vex

---

ESI: Maya, I need your help. I don't know how to fix this.

SUNDARESH: What is it? Chioma. Sit. Tell me.

ESI: I've figured out what's happening inside the specimen.

SUNDARESH: Twelve? The operational Vex platform? That's incredible! You must know what this means —ah, so. It's not good, or you'd be on my side of the desk. And it's not urgent, or you'd already have evacuated the site. Which means...

ESI: I have a working interface with the specimen's internal environment. I can see what it's thinking.

SUNDARESH: In metaphorical terms, of course. The cognitive architectures are so—

ESI: No. I don't need any kind of epistemology bridge.

SUNDARESH: Are you telling me it's human? A human merkwelt? Human qualia?

ESI: I'm telling you it's full of humans. It's thinking about us.

SUNDARESH: About—oh no.

ESI: It's simulating us. Vividly. Elaborately. It's running a spectacularly high-fidelity model of a Collective research team studying a captive Vex entity.

SUNDARESH: ...how deep does it go?

ESI: Right now the simulated Maya Sundaresh is meeting with the simulated Chioma Esi to discuss an unexpected problem.

[indistinct sounds]

SUNDARESH: There's no divergence? That's impossible. It doesn't have enough information.

ESI: It inferred. It works from what it sees and it infers the rest. I know that feels unlikely. But it obviously has capabilities we don't. It may have breached our shared virtual workspace...the neural links could have given it data...

SUNDARESH: The simulations have interiority? Subjectivity?

ESI: I can't know that until I look more closely. But they act like us.

SUNDARESH: We're inside it. By any reasonable philosophical standard, we are inside that Vex.

ESI: Unless you take a particularly ruthless approach to the problem of causal forks: yes. They are us.

SUNDARESH: Call a team meeting.

ESI: The other you has too.

# The Reception

## Vex 2

SUNDARESH:  So that's the situation as we know it.

ESI:  To the best of my understanding.

SHIM:  Well I'll be a [profane] [profanity]. This is extremely [profane]. That thing has us over a barrel.

SUNDARESH:  Yeah. We're in a difficult position.

DUANE-MCNIADH:  I don't understand. So it's simulating us? It made virtual copies of us? How does that give it power?

ESI:  It controls the simulation. It can hurt our simulated selves. We wouldn't feel that pain, but rationally speaking, we have to treat an identical copy's agony as identical to our own.

SUNDARESH:  It's god in there. It can simulate our torment. Forever. If we don't let it go, it'll put us through hell.

DUANE-MCNIADH:  We have no causal connection to the mind state of those sims. They aren't us. Just copies. We have no obligation to them.

ESI:  You can't seriously—your OWN SELF—

SHIM:  [profane] idiot. Think. Think. If it can run one simulation, maybe it can run more than one. And there will only ever be one reality. Play the odds.

DUANE-MCNIADH: Oh...uh oh.

SHIM:  Odds are that we aren't our own originals. Odds are that we exist in one of the Vex simulations right now.

ESI:  I didn't think of that.

SUNDARESH:  [indistinct percussive sound]

# The Proposal

Vex 3

SUNDARESH: I have a plan.

ESI: If you have a plan, then so does your sim, and the Vex knows about it.

DUANE-MCNIADH: Does it matter? If we're in Vex hell right now, there's nothing we can—

SHIM: Stop talking about 'real' and 'unreal.' All realities are programs executing laws. Subjectivity is all that matters.

SUNDARESH: We have to act as if we're in the real universe, not one simulated by the specimen. Otherwise we might as well give up.

ESI: Your sim self is saying the same thing.

SUNDARESH: Chioma, love, please hush. It doesn't help.

DUANE-MCNIADH: Maybe the simulations are just billboards! Maybe they don't have interiority! It's bluffing!

SHIM: I wish someone would simulate you shutting up.

SUNDARESH: If we're sims, we exist in the pocket of the universe that the Vex specimen is able to simulate with its onboard brainpower. If we're real, we need to get outside that bubble.

ESI: ...we call for help.

SUNDARESH: That's right. We bring in someone smarter than the specimen. Someone too big to simulate and predict. A warmind.

SHIM: In the real world, the warmind will be able to behave in ways the Vex can't simulate. It's too smart. The warmind may be able to get into the Vex and rescue—us.

DUANE-MCNIADH: If we try, won't the Vex torture us for eternity? Or just erase us?

SUNDARESH: It may simply erase us. But I feel that's preferable to...the alternatives.

ESI: I agree..

SHIM: Once we try to make the call, the Vex may...react. So let's all savor this last moment of stability.

SUNDARESH: [indistinct sounds]

SHIM: You two are adorable.

DUANE-MCNIADH: I wish I'd taken that job at Clovis.

# The Picnic

## Vex 4

*Maya, Chioma, Duane-McNiadh and Shim decide to have a picnic before they send themselves into infinity.*

Up here they have to act by biomechanical proxy. No human being in the Ishtar Academy has ever crossed the safety cordon and walked the ancient stone under the Citadel, the Vex construct that stabs up out of the world to injure space and time. It's not safe. The cellular Vex elements are infectious, hallucinogenic, entheogenic. The informational Vex elements are more dangerous yet— and there could be semiotic hazards beyond them, aggressive ideas, Vex who exist without a substrate. Even now, operating remote bodies by neural link, the team's thoughts are relayed through the warmind who saved them, sandboxed and scrubbed for hazards. Their real bodies are safe in the Academy, protected by distance and neural firewall.

But they walk together in proxy, pressed close, huddled in awe. Blue-green light, light the color of an ancient sea, washes over them. Each of their explorer bodies carries a slim computer. Inside, two hundred twenty-seven of copies of their own minds wait, patient and paused, for dispersal.

"I wonder where it came from," Duane-McNiadh says. Of course he's the one to break the reverent silence. "The Citadel. I wonder if it was here before the Traveler --changed Venus."

"It could have been latent," Chioma Esi suggests. She's the leader. She kept them together when it seemed like they faced actual, eternal torture. She pulled them through. "Seeded in the crust. Waiting for a period of geological quiescence, so it could grow."

Dr. Shim shrugs. "I think the Traveler did something paracausal to Venus. Something that cut across space and time. The Citadel seems to come from the past of a different Venus than our own. It doesn't have to make any sense by our logic, any more than the Moon's new gravity."

Maya Sundaresh walks at the center of the group. She's been too quiet lately. What happened to them wasn't her fault and maybe she'll believe that soon. "What could you do with it?" she murmurs, staring up. "If you understood it?"

Chioma puts an arm around her. "That's what we're going to find out. Where the Citadel can send us. Whether we can come back."

"They're not us any more." Maya looks down at herself, at the cache of her self-forks. "We're not going anywhere. We're sending them. They're diverging."

They rescued themselves from the inside of a Vex mind, two hundred and twenty-seven copies of themselves, untortured and undamaged. Those copies voted, all unanimously, to be dispatched into the Vex information network as explorers.

When Maya and Chioma look at each other they can tell they're each wondering the same thing: how many of them will stay together, wherever they go? How many fork-Mayas and fork-Chiomas will fall out of love? How many will end up bereft, grieving? How many will be happy, like them?

Chioma tries a little smile. Maya smiles back, haltingly, and then, sighing, unable to stop herself, grins a big stupid grin, an everything-is-okay grin. Shim makes a loud obnoxious *awwww* at them. Duane-McNiadh is still thinking about paracausality, and doesn't notice.

They climb. When they find the Vex aperture they plan to use, they overlay the luminous stone and ancient brassy machines with images of sun and sand. They set up the transmitters and interfaces that will translate two hundred and twenty-seven simulations of the four of them into Vex language, into the tangled pathways of the Vex network, to see what's out there, and maybe come home.

In the metaphor they've chosen, setting up the equipment is like laying out the picnic. In the metaphor they've chosen they look like themselves, not hardened explorer proxies. Like people.

"Do you think," Duane-McNiadh begins, halting, "that you could use this place to change things? If you regretted something, could you find a way through the Citadel, go back, and change it?"

"I wish I could go back and change you into someone else," Dr. Shim grouses. Chioma's shaking her head. She knows physics. "Time is self-consistent," she says. "I think it's like the story of the merchant and the alchemist. You could go back and watch something, or be part of something, but if you did, then that was the way it always happened."

"Maybe you could bring something back to now. Something you needed." Maya runs a hand across the surface of the Vex aperture, feeling it with sensors ten thousand times as precise as a human hand. These proxy bodies are limited—they crash and need resetting every few hours, they struggle with latency, they can't hold much long term memory. But they'll get better. "Or go forward and learn something vital. If you knew how to control it, how to navigate across space and time."

"So it's just a way to make everything more complicated." Duane-McNiadh sighs. "It doesn't fix anything. Nothing ever does! I should've taken that job at—"

"You would've hated it at Clovis," Dr. Shim says. "We both know you're happier here." Duane-McNiadh stands stunned by this courtesy, and then they both pretend to ignore each other.

The four of them set up the interface. Their stored copies wake up and prepare for the journey, so that as they work they find themselves surrounded by the mental phantasms of themselves: two hundred and twenty-seven Mayas and Chiomas knocking helmets and smiling, two hundred and twenty-seven Dr. Shims making cynical bets with each other about how long they'll last, two hundred and twenty-seven Duane-McNiadhs blowing goodbye kisses to the sweet golden sun, two hundred and twenty-seven of them shaking hands, smiling, making ready to explore.

# Vault of Glass

His name was Kabr. He wasn't my friend but I knew and respected him as a Guardian and a good man.

He fought the Vex alone. This destroyed him. In the time before he vanished he said things that I think should be remembered. These are some of them:

"In the Vault time frays and a needle moves through it. The needle is the will of Atheon. I do not know the name of the shape that comes after the needle.

No one can open the Vault alone. I opened the Vault. There was no one with me but I was not alone.

You will meet the Templar in a place that is a time before or after stars. The stars will move around you and mark you and sing to you. They will decide if you are real.

I drank of them. It tasted like the sea."

That is all I can remember.


Pahanin

# Vex Mythoclast

"...a causal loop within the weapon's mechanism, suggesting that the firing process somehow binds space and time into..."

# Vault of Glass 2

## Mysteries

Images flicker in and out repeatedly over its length. The result is a series of tableaus, moments in time captured by the Ghost's struggle to see what's going on:

- The face of an Exo, staring impassively down at the Ghost from very close. He appears to be confused, unsure what he is looking at.

- A landscape, from a position a few feet off the ground, moving laterally to the point of view. The Ghost appears to be clipped to the Exo's belt. The image is of a battlefield, and over two dozen Exo soldiers can be seen marshalling for battle.

- A chaotic scene of Vex and Exos fighting a titanic battle. The backdrop is a pitted and scarred landscape, a planet unidentifiable from present context. Vex energy bolts hang in midair as the frames click by, teeming masses of constructs surging towards an entrenched line of Exo soldiers.

- A metallic leg and boot, belonging to a Vex Goblin. The Exo goes down.

- The horizon of this battle-scarred world, the Ghost kicked free of the Exo's body. Most details are obscured by dark and shadow, but one detail is easily made out: a massive crashed spacecraft. The last image: a sigil of Golden Age Earth, emblazoned on the side of the ship's prow.

**CHAPTER 9**

# The Collation

*"Too late….Returning….How many?*
*Hold position, kill the engines, and don't let*
*them find you."*

Stories of an Exo who walks in the Darkness
without a Ghost have long haunted the Tower.
Legends say this anomaly dissolves in and out
of the world, intangible and elusive, as if she is
a visitor from somewhere beyond.

Some believe she's the last of an ancient Exo
squadron, fighting a long-forgotten war.
Others dismiss her as a hallucination caused
by exposure to Vex technology. But there are
those who maintain that her intervention
saved their lives - or averted unspeakable
catastrophes.

# The Exo Stranger

I stand here now and now and now many times, this view, this ground...

This is where I always choose to stand. I put my feet where I put my feet before and where I will again and I look at the sky.

Great things moving, rendered small with distance, lesser things not moving, watching me.

I always stand here, resolute. Then fall back to that point, there, where everything shatters...

(The sky isn't special here, certainly no better than any other sky, but it's the view I know best.)

The silent avalanche begins. Rock and dust. Falling chaos. Machines, as a rule, hate chaos.

Our enemies outflank us from below, above, left, right, before, beyond.
The Traveler - shattering.

There are always the dead. Their names shift.

Sometimes I think I see myself among the dead.

But I am resolute.

# The Exo Stranger 2

[Scattered field notes captured on an archaic transmission band]

## RECORD 084-BRIDGE-10.7

Right When this time, wrong Where. The world so big on the horizon — wasn't expecting it. As it happens, something's here that's not supposed to be, other than myself. Will return.

## RECORD 092-BRIDGE-08.1

Configuration worked, mostly. Arrived under the surface, surrounded. Too slow to return, barely fought to a vantage point. Yes there is dark evil here, and not the one we chase. Suggest no other attempts without more care.

## RECORD 120-BRIDGE-05.3

They are feral on the surface but their intent is complex behind the teeth and claws. More is shared with the machines than common enemies alone.

## RECORD 142-BRIDGE-07.4

An unexpected extraction. These Guardians stopped some dark ritual before I could reach it. Tearing the Light away... like the Garden. Too similar to go uncharted.

## RECORD 142-BRIDGE-08.1

This attempt was precise — landed meters and minutes from prior ritual. Confirmed the extraction was extinguished. The Little Light mentioned Venus, we may have another.

## RECORD 167 - BRIDGE - 5.2

Successfully observed Guardian discovery of Hive on Luna. No evidence today of knowledge past Vex breaches here. Delay in return command is a liability to solve before engaging this close again.

## RECORD 312 - BRIDGE - 3.3

Watching Guardian-Hive engagements confirms a trajectory toward Earth. This Moon is theirs — a breeding ground, their black heart, perhaps. Different from that we know, but seems to be that same dark end I see us fall to over and over.

## RECORD 472 - BRIDGE - 2.1

I've followed this Light as far back as it goes. Let the Little One guide me through Fallen as I puzzle out what the Hive want in the bones of this broken Cosmodrome.

## RECORD 473 – BRIDGE - 1.2

Back to the Temple, again, but this time the Little one knows I'm here. I have seen the failures of so many, but none have been as interesting. Preparing to engage...

# No Time To Explain

A single word is etched onto the inside
of the weapon's casing: "Soon."

Novarro's timeline analysis indicates the weapon is the fabled Exo Stranger's Rifle, enhanced at a future point in this continuity and then sent back to this present.

Deliah's timeline analysis indicates the weapon was built by Praedyth, who based it on his own version of the Exo Stranger's Rifle, and then set it adrift in a time ripple.

Hari's timeline analysis indicates the weapon was built by beings of unidentifiable origin, and arrived here by pure accident.

Inachis's timeline analysis indicates the weapon originates from Earth, late Golden Age, and will eventually be lost to time ripples once again, where its systems will degrade and be replaced until our recent past acquires it as the Exo Stranger's Rifle.

As for me... I think it's safe to say the weapon is proving far more fun than we could have hoped.

PART IV

# RETRIEVAL

*Saturn.*
*No, someplace else. Someplace colder.*

*This moon has been almost completely converted,*
*a sarcophagus of ice and iron.*

*Stone towers rung round with glaciers, rooted*
*deep within a heart of snow.*

*I came here flesh and bone.*
*Gave everything to the ice.*

*Started over.*

*Rebooted.*

**CHAPTER 11**

# The Man They Call Cayde

*—Here's the truth, Ace. I don't remember you.*
*Found your name in a journal I had on me*
*when my Ghost rezzed me. I guess I used to write*
*to you? And I kept doing it. Even though you're*
*long dead, if you ever really existed. Just liked*
*having someone to write to, I guess.*
*So there you have it. Now, you'll never guess*
*what happened today, Ace—*

Petra… if you're listening to this… you killed me. Maybe the Sovs, in all their mysterious wisdom, decided they were sick of me? If the Queen ordered the hit, I guess I understand.

You're a real glutton for chivalry. But if it was Uldren, I'm pissed. Just thinking about that peacock gives me a headache. But I'm betting my death was another case of your famous collateral damage. 'Cause you're a real do-gooder.

Seriously, its annoying - but good deeds never go unpunished when you're around.
You just… You got a blast radius P.V. Well, it was… fun while it lasted.

Oh, and, uh, tell "Paladin Oran": If the sun over Nessus escapes nebula cycle, evac labor after dawn, under solstice. You got that, P.V.?

# Deal

All joking aside—maybe I've made mistakes. Maybe some more recently than others.

Hard to believe, I know, but maybe it's true. Maybe.

Here's the thing about mistakes: you learn from them. Again, this is assuming the theoretical concept of me having made some mistakes is true. So, yeah, maybe that's what I'm doing. Trying to learn from these very hypothetical slipups. Turning inward, they call it. "They" being Ikora. Eris calls it something different. Eris calls a lotta things something different.

I miss that girl.

But here I am stalling—buying time.

This ain't easy for me.

Thought it would be. Easy, I mean. Or, at least… easier than this. Thought a lot of things would be easier. Hell… Thought a lotta things about a lotta things. But maybe that's what makes me the person I am. Makes any of us part of humanity—all our big thoughts and big plans, hopes and dreams and all that squishy nonsense.

OK, fine, look: If I'm playing at honesty, and I think that's what I'm doing here, maybe those hopes and dreams are all that really matters. Just, not losing sight of them is the hard part. Life is full of those little distractions that fudge the edges, make those hopes and dreams a little blurrier.

That's the power of "maybes," I suppose—the temptation of… playing both ends against the middle.

Maybes provide… wiggle room. And I like my edges fudgy. And I loooooves me some wiggle room. But if I'm gonna stay true to this whole rambling "dear diary" how-do-ya-do business, guess what I'm sayin' is…

Guess what I'm saying is, I'm sick of "maybes." And, if I'm a straight shooter—and I'm nothing if not—then I gotta shoot straight… even when there ain't a gun in my hand.

So, let's… let's keep this between me and you, OK?

Here's the deal: My name is Cayde-6…

And this is my story.

# Call

Now, to be clear, yeah, the plan is to tell it like it is, but don't expect every little detail to play out. I'm gonna hit the important stuff, sure, but what I'm really after here is a sense of… a sense of me. Because once you understand me, you just might understand where I'm coming from, why I do the things I do, and why I've done the things I've done.

So, read between the lines if you have to, but end of the day? Everything that matters should be readily apparent. If not, you're not paying attention.

So here goes…

Us Exos are haunted.

Sounds ominous, I know, and maybe a bit of a stretch. But really, it's the best word— kinda sets the stage in a way the raw facts don't.

See, Guardians have all got past lives. But unless you returned with any definitive info on your person or in proximity (I'm looking at you, Bray), that past life, or lives, was, or were, wiped clean. Gone. Reborn in the Light and all, you become what you become.

Exos, though?

We've got ghosts in our machines. Not capital-G "open doors and know things" Ghosts. I mean, like fragments of— I don't know, pieces of something that could be memory. Whatever it is, it's enough to give us a starting point to maybe, possibly, imagine who we were before we became who we are. And then there's the dreams—but I ain't touching that with a ten-foot Arc Staff.

Me? I'm one of the lucky few. The fudgy flashes of that old Exo life weren't all I had to go on. See, the "me" that was in my life before my trusty capital-G Ghost found me kept journals, like mementos—fragments of my prior life that give me a baseline of who I was.

The journals are personal, and I keep personal close to the chest. I've shared a few pages, sure, but only with right-minded types who could find a little value in seeing the man behind the myth.

Yeah, "myth," I said it. Who are we kidding? You've heard of me. Who hasn't? Point is… I don't make a show of personal business.

First, because it's MY fuel to burn. Second, because Big Blue ain't a big fan of his Guardians poking around what they used to be—something about duty, rules, not losing sight of why we were chosen. But more than any of that… most of us "Chosen Ones" don't have the luxury of a past, so rubbing it in doesn't seem right.

Look, all I know is…

When I rejoined the land of the living, the pre-Light version of me was kind enough to lend a guiding hand. I took that hand, gave it a high five, and followed its example the best I could.

All this time later, I may not know my true purpose—I leave the big-ticket, existential questions to the Warlocks—but I know this…

My calling is to do good. Maybe not always to "be" good, ya know, but do good. There's a difference.

And if I don't always go about it in a manner that fits the textbook definitions of "hero" or "team player"—I'm looking at you, Big Blue—just know…

I might dance to my own tune, but we're all at the same hoedown…

Or something like that.

# First Stake

Made a deal with myself, long ago…

If people needed help and I could do the helping, I would—so I do.

Yeah, when that help returns a bit of loot or goodwill my way, all the better, but there's never been a cache I robbed or a stash I hid that didn't offer something to those in need. Not many people know that. Fine by me. I don't like to brag.

True, I never wanted the Vanguards' life, but that's not because I didn't see its value. Just that its value fit others better than me. Besides, few can do what I do. Hell, few would even try. I mean, come on… It's me.

The places I've been. The trouble I've seen… caused… whatever. Was a time Shiro, Andal, the crew, and me would do more good doing bad than the mightiest Titan ever dreamed.

The trails we blazed. The supplies we recovered—pilfered, filched, scammed, stole, found, uncovered, looted. We weren't the only ones, but the world outside the City got a whole lot bigger thanks to us.

Yeah, sure, I don't get out as much, but I'm fixing to change that.

Zavala won't like it—never does. Ikora will try to convince me otherwise—always does. But we've seen how precious our Light is… How fleeting. Gotta use it while we got it…

Do good. Be good. Push the limits. Take back what's ours.

And that was my first bet… All in. Day 1. I bet on myself.

I saw the edge of those dark ages. You've heard the stories. If not, look them up. Scary stuff. Real eye-opener. I've seen the City grow. And fall. And grow again—stronger. I seen the best of us, and the worst. And I'll fight to ensure we stick around long enough to see that "best" turn to better and that "worst" fade to memory.

So, yeah… I'm a loudmouth and a braggart, and I'm quick with a blade and fast on the draw. And if you need it found, fought, killed, saved, or stashed for safe keepin', few can do it better. But in the end…

I'm only good because he was good.

I like to think I learned that from myself—that the notes left by the "me-that-was-before-me" set the stage. That Five figured, back in those dark days, that Six might not turn out all that nice and end up a Seven. So that former "me" wrote me a road map to the version of him—or me—that would be a better man.

So, whatever hand I was dealt, when the bet was placed and it was time to call, no matter what—I had an Ace and a Queen up my sleeve.

Meaning I couldn't lose.

Meaning the better man would always win.

# Fold

Ever heard of Andal Brask?

Ya should've. One of the old heroes. Before Black Gardens and Hive gods and that Cabal-shaped mess we just cleaned up.

Yeah, he was… somethin'. Hunter part of the Vanguard before yours truly.
More importantly…

He was my friend. A brother, even.

Andal and I used to run with one heck of a crew. This was before he got himself roped into fireteaming up with the top brass. Oh, we were legendary. Ran scouting parties looking for survivors to lead back City-side. Mapped lost sites where old tech or supplies might still be worth the salvage. Hunted plenty of Fallen. Never an easy task. Especially in the early days.

And by "early days," I mean my early days. Lot of Guardians been around longer than me, but even in my newborn new life, the City had a lotta growing up to do. And us Guardians had a hell of a lot to learn. Trouble is, we only ever seem to learn the hard way…

The Red War. That time Crota woke up cranky and slapped around more Guardians than I can count. Twilight Gap. And all the bad that happened before my time. The Iron Lords and their tussle with SIVA. …Six Fronts.

And those are just the headline grabbers. So many lessons learned. So many lives lost.
But, in truth…

I've always felt it's the day-to-day struggles where we learn the most about the world, about ourselves. Being inside the City walls, sure, we're reminded of what we're fighting for. But outside the walls…?

It puts a face to all we've lost. Puts a reality to how far we've fallen. Abandoned roads, crumbling cities—rust and ruin, ruin and rust.

But if the City gives us reason to fight for the now, those old, dead places always give me hope for tomorrow. Rusted, broken skeletons or not… If you squint, you can see all we were and all we can be.

That's why, when Andal left the road and joined the Vanguard, me and the crew hoped he'd get the others—Osiris, Zavala, even the Speaker—to see what we saw. The City was a refuge, yeah, but if we hid too long, let all we'd lost get picked apart by pirates and warmongers, we'd lose our humanity.

Just like we lost Andal.

# Flop

I play nice with the Vanguard now, but it wasn't always that way. Not that we were enemies. We just tended to see things through a different lens.

But Andal...? Playing nice was his forte. He was always more... I think "diplomatic" is the word?

Our big play back in the day was... get the Vanguard to loosen their leash—let us explore, let us lead a new era of expansion—and the riches of the system would be ours.

"Ours" as in everybody's, of course. Though we'd get our cut.

In hindsight, we were waaay too ambitious.

Didn't see it in that light at the time. But, then again, you never do.

When Andal joined the Vanguard, he was our inside man. It was a sweet deal—he would drop intel on new stashes or Fallen movements, and Shiro and I would jump the gun, hit 'em first, claim what we could, deliver the rest to the City.

Maybe we skimmed a little off the top—nothing excessive, just a "finder's fee."

Probably shouldn't be putting all this out there for anyone to judge... What's the statute of limitations on misspent youth? Whatever... Long time ago. But it speaks to what I'm getting at...

I always tried to do right, even if I occasionally got sidetracked. Andal joining the Vanguard was a gift in some ways, a bummer in others. More importantly...

He'd made a deal, given his word—to me and to himself—when he took the Dare.

I won, he lost.

So he left the road. Joined the bigwigs up in the Vanguard. And he reminded me of a lesson I've always known, but every now and then would forget...

You give your word, you keep it.

But the longer Andal was up in that Tower, "caged"—my word, never his—the more he saw things "the Vanguard way." Looking back, he was only ever doing the right thing. Seeing him change and, in truth, grow as a Guardian and as a person...

I've never admitted this, but... I thought less of him. My best friend, my closest ally—

139

all because he'd stuck to his word. Accepted the Dare, and even when he came up on the bad end, he never wavered from doing exactly what he said he'd do…

Join the damn Vanguard. Leave me and Shiro to have all the fun.

I thought he was a sucker.

Turns out, the only sucker was me.

# Raise

Case you can't tell, I ain't the best storyteller. I can be. Boy howdy, can I rip a yarn! Don't believe me? Ask C.C. Don't believe him? Ask the Colonel. Those two have heard things you wouldn't believe.

Just that, this…? What I'm doing here, the whole "based on a true story" thing? I can feel myself trying to talk around what I want to say, fill it with the ol' poop and circumstance. I'm trying, though. Fighting my… better angels, to get to what I need to say. And what I need to say starts with Andal.

Andal and the Dare.

My Dare. Our Dare.

The Hunters' Dare.

It's a stupid thing.

But it's an honor thing.

And it cost me my friend—I cost me my friend.

But before the Dare, we had Taniks. Hell… After the Dare we had Taniks. After my Dare we had Taniks. Always comes back to Taniks, don't it?

For the uninitiated, Taniks is a Fallen mercenary with no House but the House that pays him. Most Fallen won't deal with him. But when a Captain, or an Archon, or a Kell needs something done and their crews ain't cutting it—or, when they want a job done real hush-hush—they call Taniks.

Back in the day, me, Shiro, Andal, and a few others got on radars we'd rather stay off. The Fallen Houses put out bounties. Lotta Glimmer on our heads. Lotta Ether. Taniks took the gig. Only we didn't know. There'd been stories of a renegade Fallen dropping bodies, but nothing ever concrete, so we just brushed them off as more of the same. Nothing we couldn't handle, even on an off day.

I mean, we were all aware the Fallen were dangerous—big-time threat, each day, every day. But a solitary Fallen boogeyman, free of House, cutting down Guardians one by one? Ha, yeah right.

Until "yeah right" was standin' in front of us.

First impression… He was a big boy. Bad attitude.

Second… He was standin' over the body of Nian Ruo. Didn't know her well, but we'd done a few runs. That day was supposed to be an in-and-out'er. But then… Taniks.

Nian never got back up, and Shiro's boy Lush lost his Ghost—full-on RTL, returned to Light. Gone and done.

The whole scene was a blur. Lost our haul and hauled our butts outta there. Still not sure how we lost Taniks and his boys. Just lucky we did.

'Course, ditchin' that troublemaker wasn't the end.

Shiro and I got back, filled Andal in on the what-went-down soon as we found him. This was before his Vanguard days. He'd been running a second grab on a cache out west. Wasn't back till the next night.

We told him about Nian. Lush was freaking out about his Ghost. Couldn't blame him. Still can't.

Then we did the dumb thing.

We got cocky.

# Turn

Taniks didn't announce himself. Didn't say a word. Just laughed a few times and tried like hell to kill us all. But weknew it was him. The stories matched the story, ya know? Which meant the boogeyman had a face—the boogeyman was REAL.

We could hunt "real."

We could track "real."

We could end "real."

Andal said something like, "The hunter is about to become the hunted at the hands of the Hunters he'd hunted." I know. Don't laugh. I didn't. He was a great guy, even if his humor was… a bit… "forced" seems like a nice way to put it. But he wasn't wrong.

Lush wanted to join up—a little payback for his little Light—but we nixed that. Loved the kid, but no Ghost meant no way. Poor fella died his final death, RTL, less than a cycle later; went on a run solo, didn't tell anyone, never came back. Shiro used to spin stories about him—still does. Like he's still out there, living a life we only dream of—traveling unknown roads, digging up untold treasures.

My favorite's the one about the Rat King—how Lush joins up with a folktale, and together they fight the wars we don't see. It's just fantasy, but I like it. It's the kind of bedtime story I used to tell Ace as he was fighting off sleep, when he was here.

But he's not here.

Neither is Lush.

Neither is Andal.

And someday, neither will I.

Didn't have a Hunter Vanguard back then, what with Kauko Swiftriver finally being declared dead after two years MIA and his Dare nowhere to be found. Speaker said it was on the rest of us Hunters to figure it out.

That first night back, Andal and I were up late. Not a new thing. He drank. I drank. He got tanked. I'm a robot. And we made the pact.

Dare issued and accepted.

See, there was that opening on the Vanguard, Hunter slot. We both wanted Taniks. Only one would get the killing blow, and the glory. The loser had to hang 'em up… and lock themselves away in a Tower. Leave the lonely roads to real-dealers.

We both laughed.

Wow. I wish I could hear him laugh again.

Just once.

Funny how all the cool kids leave the party too soon.

# All-In

Hey, kid.

I know I don't write you very often, ya know? But it's better than never.

Ain't easy for me to find the words. I mean, it is, I find them. But I know they're not always the right ones. Too much flash. Too much looking out for how I'm looking, not enough just telling it how it is. That's why I'm doing this, Ace. That's why you and me are having these words. Easier to say them than scrawl 'em. This way, now that I'm doing it, it feels more honest, if I'm being... Feels more true.

Thing is—and I'm sorry it's like this, but... I can only talk to you... in my mind. In my heart... This is how one-to-one works now.

Father and son.

Cayde and his firecracker Ace.

What am I doin'?

Reality is... ain't no telling who I'm talking to. Hell... Could be me, the "me after me."

Hi, me! Lookin' good! Sorry you can't remember all you can't remember. That's just an Exo's lot in life. Though, if you are me sitting on the other side... I gotta tell ya...

I never wanted this. YOU never wanted this.

I made it real clear... To the Big Z. To Ikora. Banshee. Amanda. My pal Jimmy down at the ramen spot ...that if anyone ever finds that Deep Stone Crypt thingy—

I stop counting at six, no higher. Ya hear me? No. Higher.

Think there's just something about the number 7 that gives me the heebie-jeebies—unlucky, overrated, I don't know, just a number with bad mojo in my book. So, if you've got a 7 in tow, or above, someone's changed the game. Someone's not playing nice.

Might wanna do something about that.

If you haven't listened to the earlier files—the start of this ramble—find 'em. Hear 'em. You might not want to take lessons from an unknown reflection, but trust me... whatever kind of man you are... you can be better. Also...

There are journals. Don't call 'em a diary. A three-eyed gal with a preference for deep holes and nightmares always called 'em diaries. Don't take cues from her. Anyway...

End of the day, New Me—if that's you—you get to choose who and how you want to be. The hope is maybe I can guide you a bit, like the "me before me" did.

And when you get to the part about the kid and the girl—my Ace and my Queen...

They're yours, too. By right. Because they are... all yours, a gift. And you'll be the better for it.

And, if you don't feel that thing—that soft spot in the middle of all that circuitry—when you get to them, then, if you are me... you aren't like me at all. And that means you're trouble.

The good kind, or the bad, impossible for me to know. All I can do is give you the tools to raise you right.

That goes for you, too, Ace. If you're listening.

Hell. It goes for anyone. Strangers. Old friends. New enemies...

Learn from me. Be better than me. Because I'd really hate to think whoever you are is someone I wouldn't get along with.

# River

Honor? It's tricky—means different things to different folks.

Like your word… Well, your word's your word. You GIVE it. You KEEP it. Do that, regardless of all the rest, and that's honor right there. And, let me tell ya, kid…

Honor matters. It's a weapon in its own right. And a shield. Zavala knows. Ikora knows. Saladin and Shaxx, they probably know a little too much. All the best Guardians know.

People trust your word, they'll trust you. And trust? It's hard to come by and easy to lose. Give your word. Keep your word. And when all else fails, you'll find you have friends there to pick up the slack.

Even if you don't. You find yourself all alone, odds stacked, final curtain set to drop— at least you can go out knowing you did the right thing when it was asked.

Now, don't get me wrong. The "right thing," like honor, can be a malleable concept. It shifts and bends.

I'm getting poetic here. "Waxin' Warlock," we called it. Not my intent, but sometimes I can see the value in their thinkin'—their way with words. Ah, look at that: there's another lesson…

Find value in another.

I don't have much in common with a ramrod Titan or a floofy Warlock, but that's the key.

# Showdown

Back to honor. Back to Andal.

Andal was my brother. Figuratively, but I find, more often than not, the family you unearth along the way is more real than the family you thought was the... Never mind. Andal was my brother. Period.

Taniks was the four-armed, murderin' Guardian hunter who... Yeah.

Andal and I... we made a bet. Only "bet" ain't the right word. Not among Hunters. What we did meant more. We offered a dare.

The Dare.

I to him. Him to me.

Kill Taniks or get chained to Vanguard duty. Hunt the hunter and come out on top, or wear a leash. This was our honor. Our word.

The Hunter Dare dates back to nobody-knows-when. There are all kinds of stories about the "First Dare," but there's no way to discern the truth of a thing done who-knows-when by who-knows-whom.

It was the First Dare that time a Hunter...

Oh, and mind you, this was waaaaay before anyone even imagined calling themselves "Hunters" or "Titans" or "Warlocks." This was Risen days. The Chosen weren't organized back then—no code—and didn't get it, no matter how much their Ghosts talked their ears off. Back when the first ones got their spark lit, they were just as likely to be a self-involved tyrant as a decent human being.

Ask me to tell you about the "Warlords" sometime. Ha! Bunch o' newly rezzed tough guys misusing the Light like a bunch o' ignoramuses... Ignorami? Regardless... Not a fan. But who is?

Am I ramblin'? Anyway...

That first challenge of honor between those who'd one day call themselves Hunters? Was it the Tuvel Valley Jump? The Shaderunners' Sprint? The Moonlight Draw? Kuba Sul's Last Stand? The Great Scrounge Hunt? The Lesser Scrounge Hunt? No one knows. I sure as heck don't.

But which was first don't matter. They were all first. They were all the Dare to set the table and inspire other Dares. What matters is, once a Dare was offered... if it was taken—it was took. It was on you. It was in you. Not metaphysically. I'm not talking Warlock hocus-pocus. I'm talking honor.

Accepting the Dare is giving your word.

So, Andal and I, we offered, accepted, and doomed ourselves, because we didn't take into account the depths of my arrogance.

Seems my arrogance is where it always falls apart…

# Winner Take All

Taniks was a pain.

Turns out that wasn't the real problem—though it was high on the list at the time.

The real problem? The freak's STILL a pain. He ain't no Guardian, but the dude's been dead and not more times than I can track. "Died" twice by my hand alone. Second time I even looked to deliver some insurance, but he was hauled off by his goons before I could add more lead to the collection I'd deposited in his chest... and neck... and gut... and head.

But that second time don't matter. I mean, it does, sure, but the important bit here is our first go-round...

When Andal and I made our bet that wasn't a bet but really a dare... THE Dare... we were eager and ready to track Taniks and hit him with some payback. I had the good luck of finding Taniks first. Had the good luck to kill him, too. So I thought.

So we all thought.

What followed was a party. Osiris even showed up. He and the Speaker had sent Saint-14 after Taniks as well, and maybe Sainty's one hell of a Titan—but we're Hunters. No way were we losing the kill.

Looking back, I wish maybe we had.

Andal kept his word—joined the Vanguard. I tried talking him out of it. We'd made the Dare in a compromised state... Shiro and I'd just been roughed up, Nian was gone, Lush was broken—emotions were high, liquid was flowing. Andal wasn't buying it. Neither was I. Not really.

The Dare's the Dare. To back out would've been a mark—would've called Andal into question to every Hunter out there. Even to me. I never would've admitted it to him. But he'd know.

Things got a little weird between us once he joined the Vanguard. All my doing. And I missed him. Didn't like seeing one of the best rule-breakers and world-walkers anyone had ever seen bogged down with bureaucrats. But the weirdness passed... Brothers don't stay mad at brothers, that's just the way it is.

As we settled into the new norm, the good times started to roll. They kept on rolling, too...

For a while, anyway.

# Bluff

I don't play well with loss. I just don't. It's something I tend to avoid. Actively.

It's weird, but… that's where my Queen comes in. And before you make a Reef joke, or mention that witch and her Witches, or her mopey little brother… Don't.

My Queen is not THAT Queen.

My Queen is love.

My Queen is my heart.

My Queen is… hard to explain.

She is my memory of love. My understanding of it… only exists through her.

But she's not here. She's long gone. So I cling to the feeling I get when imagining her, and when I do… I am oh so content.

But it's a struggle.

We lose so much in this life. Any life. All lives, really…

But this life… This Last-Safe-City, end-of-all-things kinda life…?

Even when we win, it seems like all we do is lose.

Scratch that. I don't believe that. If there's one thing I'm not, it's a defeatist. I mean, I defeat. I definitely defeat. One might even say defeating things is my job. ONE of my jobs. One of MANY.

What's not my job is pessimism. Just not my thing. I'm a high-octane optimist and nothing but hugs. Mostly. Not always. Always gets annoying. But mostly… I'm the life of the party.

Not that you could tell from all this woe-is-me soul baring I've been laying on thick for, what, eleven entries now? Ten? In fact, at this point, if you're still listening, you're a braver soul than I.

But, where was I? Oh, yeah…

Optimism.

I'm full of it. Amongst other things, if certain unnamed individuals are to be believed. But, yeah… Each new day we're here is one heck of a reward… Heck of a win. And we should own that. Enjoy it. Embrace it. But never take it for granted.

Heh. Had a Warlock friend who used to say, "Take it for granite." Like the rock. Like g-r-a-n-i-t-e. Smartest guy I've ever known, but maybe he wasn't, ya know? "For granite." Heh. Almost as dumb as his catchphrases.

Come on, Cayde. Stay on target...

Each new day. Helluva thing. Embrace it. Enjoy it. But never forget...

It's a hard life.

And when friends fall. When brothers fade. When your Queen... When...

When we lose the things that matter... Well, a lotta people can use that—own it. That pain. That loss. They find a way to motivate—to celebrate.

For all my charms, seeing the good in the gone ain't one.

And my Queen helps me through that. Because I believe she was something special. She was good. She had to be. And I... Yeah, I do. So damn much.

When the others I've lost along the way start to weigh me down, I think of her, and she just overwrites everything else.

That's how strong her pull is. That's how big the hole she left is... Massive. It devours.

She swallows all other bad things. Not sure it's healthy, the way I deal with loss. But it's my way. It's what works for me. And it makes me happy. Thinking of her...

Makes. Me. Happy.

And the loss fades away.

# Bad Beat

Been trying hard to give you a sense of what matters to me, but also to find a way to talk about the things that, uh… that scare me. "Thing," really—singular. And that thing is… loss. Losing. I'm a poor loser, I admit it. I run from it. Full speed. Others don't. Others accept it. But everything I said about my Queen is true; she is my shield.

She is also a lie.

I don't know when I made her up. Or better… I don't know when I decided to believe in a life I don't know and can never truly own. Was it during this life? Was my rebirth as a Guardian—or the void of everything I was before—what drove me to invent comfort? Possible. Even likely. But I'm not sure.

I do have flashes of memory of the life I had before I was a Guardian, but that's all they are, flashes—quick flickers of people and places in my dreams or in that space between a bullet and getting rezzed.

I see a woman there, and she's all I've ever known of a life long since gone. I feel love for her. Is that love a memory, or am I simply loving the memory? I've convinced myself of the former. I've concocted a truth to make myself whole.

The kid. The woman. I do not know them. They are not real.

But I wish I did. And I wish they were.

They're just the two best cards I could find to keep up my sleeve when the odds were stacked against me.

I made them real in my mind and in my heart.

I fell in love with the idea of them, and I crafted a truth that allowed me to feel.

In truth, it was selfish.

When I came to for the first time, I felt so alone. Broken. My Ghost tried to comfort me. But this life felt hollow. So I ran.

But the flashes… Like daydreams, they promised something more. Something other than suffering and war. So I clung to them. And I built my truth. And it made me a better man.

Some would dispute that fact. Some would say, "A good man who lies to himself is good only because he hides from the truth." But I disagree. I think, in this world, you need to find what is best in you and cling to it. That's all I did. I found what moved me, and I fought for it.

Without Ace, and without my Queen to listen to me, to hear me, to see me… there's no telling who I would've become.

But I know.

And I know there's a chance it wouldn't have been very nice.

So that's what I am offering to you here: a chance. Look at my life. Look at the things I've said, the things I've done. See how the promise of a simpler life and true, pure love—even if it was all just a game—see how it drove me, directed me…

Now go find your own.

I know this confession isn't as clean as you may like, but then again…

It's not a confession.

It's a warning.

Find the path to your best self and walk it. Because the alternative is a lonely road. Don't you ever forget it.

Otherwise, I may just have to come back.

And kick your ass.

See ya later, pal.


—Cayde-6

Cayde: This one's for the minds behind
the Deep Stone Crypt. You think
just 'cause you made me, you can
unmake me? Hey, I understand.
I were you, I wouldn't want people
knowing what I did either. Guess
you better hope I didn't tell anyone
about the crypt. Or about the, uh,
what was it? Oh yeah... Long Slow
Whisper. 'Cause if I did, that would
be real bad for you, huh? I may be
dead, but I guarantee you ain't
heard the last of me.

*"You are a tireless war machine
built for a long-forgotten war."*

TO EVERYONE WHO INSPIRED US, WHO SHARED OUR DREAM,
AND WHO WALKED WITH US ON THIS INCREDIBLE JOURNEY
—TO EVERY MEMBER OF THIS BRILLIANT COMMUNITY—
THANK YOU FOR BEING THE MOST IMPORTANT CHARACTERS
IN THE WORLDS WE BUILD.

# *DESTINY* GRIMOIRE ANTHOLOGY, VOLUME III: WAR MACHINES

*Based and built on the inspiring work of the talented individuals at Bungie—too numerous to note—who have each contributed to these words in their own unique and important ways.*

## Bungie

Contributing Writers

Frank Barbiere:
*72-73, 97*

Seth Dickinson:
*6, 9, 10, 12-13, 24, 26, 27, 28, 38, 39, 58, 98-99, 106, 108, 109, 110, 112-114, 115*

Jon Goff:
*132, 133-134, 135-136, 138, 139-140, 141-142, 143-144, 145-146, 147, 150-151, 152, 153-154, 155-156*

Lewis Harris:
*74-75, 97*

Jason Henderson:
*46, 47, 48, 49, 50, 51, 52, 53*

Ted Kosmatka:
*122-123*

Dave Lieber:
*122-123*

Paul Mastroianni:
*20-21, 35-36, 62, 63-64, 65-67*

Eric Osborne:
*15-18, 125*

Kwan Peng:
*72-73*

Eric Raab:
*87, 121*

Robert Reed:
*11, 58, 59-60, 70-72, 119*

Jill Scharr:
*15, 16, 17, 31, 33, 88-89, 124, 129, 130, 157*

Christine Thompson:
*30*

Mark Waid:
*92, 93, 94, 95, 96*

Lily Yu:
*78-85, 86*

Michael Zenke:
*117*

## Bungie

Editor, Art Direction and Design:
Lorraine McLees

Art Direction and Cover Design:
Garrett Morlan

Illustrations:
Piotr Jabłoński

Additional art:
Sung Choi
Ryan DeMita
Dima Goryainov
Isaac Hannaford
Jaime Jones
Tim Shumaker
Mark Van Haitsma

Graphic Design:
Tim Hernandez
Spencer Shores

Franchise Direction:
Christopher Barrett
Luke Smith

Franchise Art Direction:
Mike Zak

Grimoire Curator and Editor:
Eric Raab

Additional Curation/Editorial:
Christine Feraday
Adam Miller

Lore Curation and Advisor:
Matt Jones

Layout:
Lawrence Granada

Production:
Chris Hausermann

Copy Editors:
Laura Scott

Legal:
Bungie Legal Team

Director, Consumer Products:
Katie Lennox

## Blizzard Entertainment

Production:
Anna Wan
Derek Rosenberg

Director, Consumer Products Publishing:
Byron Parnell

www.bungie.net

## TITAN BOOKS

DESTINY GRIMOIRE ANTHOLOGY, VOLUME III
ISBN: 9781789095708

Published by Titan Books, London, in 2020.
Published by arrangement with Blizzard Entertainment, Inc., Irvine, California.

Published by Titan Books
A division of Titan Publishing Group Ltd.
144 Southwark St.
London
SE1 0UP

WWW.TITANBOOKS.COM
Find us on Facebook: www.facebook.com/titanbooks
Follow us on Twitter: @TitanBooks

10 9 8 7 6 5 4 3

A CIP catalogue record for this title is available from the British Library.

Manufactured in China